27

NUCLEAR RISK REDUCTION MEASURES IN SOUTH ASIA: PROBLEMS AND PROSPECTS

The Regional Centre for Strategic Studies (RCSS) is an independent, non-profit and non-governmental organization for collaborative research, networking and interaction on strategic and international issues pertaining to South Asia. Set up in 1992, the RCSS is based in Colombo, Sri Lanka.

The RCSS is a South Asian forum for studies, training and multi-track dialogue and deliberation on issues of regional interest. All activities of RCSS are designed with a South Asia focus and are usually participated by experts from all South Asian countries. The Centre is envisaged as a forum for advancing the cause of cooperation, security, conflict resolution, confidence building, peace and development in the countries of the South Asian region.

The RCSS serves its South Asian and international constituency by: (a) networking programmes that promote interaction, communication and exchange between institutions and individuals within and outside the region engaged in South Asian strategic studies; (b) organizing regional workshops and seminars and sponsoring and coordinating collaborative research; and (c) disseminating output of the research through publications which include books, monographs and a quarterly newsletter. The RCSS facilitates scholars and other professionals of South Asia to address, mutually and collectively, problems and issues of topical interest for all countries of the region.

Queries may be addressed to:

Regional Centre for Strategic Studies
2 Elibank Road
Colombo 5
SRI LANKA
Tel: (94-11) 2599734, 2599735
Fax: 2599993; e-mail: rcss@sri.lanka.net
RCSS website: http://www.rcss.org

RCSS Policy Studies 35

Nuclear Risk Reduction Measures in South Asia: Problems and Prospects

UPENDRA CHOUDHURY

REGIONAL CENTRE FOR STRATEGIC STUDIES
COLOMBO

MANOHAR
2006

Published by
Ajay Kumar Jain for
Manohar Publishers & Distributors
4753/23 Ansari Road, Daryaganj
New Delhi 110 002
and
Regional Centre for Strategic Studies
2 Elibank Road
Colombo 5
SRI LANKA
Tel: (94-11) 2599734-5; Fax: 2599993;
e-mail: rcss@sri.lanka.net
Website: http://www.rcss.org

First published 2006

ISBN 81-7304-661-1

Typeset by
Kohli Print
Delhi 110 051

Printed at
Lordson Publishers Pvt. Ltd.
Delhi 110 007

Distributed in South Asia by
FOUNDATION BOOKS
4381/4, Ansari Rorad
Daryaganj, New Delhi 110 002
and its branches at Mumbai, Hyderabad,
Bangalore, Chennai, Kolkata

Contents

RCSS is grateful to the
Ford Foundation for its generous
support for the Kodikara Award
on which this report is based.

Acknowledgements

Many individuals and institutions helped me during the research for this book. First, I thank the Regional Centre for Strategic Studies (RCCS), Colombo, Sri Lanka, for selecting me for the Kodikara Research Award and providing necessary financial support to carry out this research.

I am thankful to my Supervisor, Lt. Gen. V. R. Raghavan (Retd.), for his valuable guidance and continuous support. I also appreciate the cooperation and cordiality of the staff of various libraries—the American Center, New Delhi; Institute for Defence Studies and Analyses, New Delhi; Jawaharlal Nehru University, New Delhi; Nehru Memorial Museum & Library, New Delhi; United Service Institution of India, New Delhi; and Maulana Azad Library, Aligarh Muslim University, Aligarh—for helping me in collecting material for this project.

Words are not sufficient to express my feelings of gratitude to my wife, Fani, daughter Abhipsa, and son Akshyat, whose patience, sacrifice and assistance helped me greatly in preparing this project. I also acknowledge my gratitude to my parents and other family members for their constant support and encouragement.

Finally, I would like to thank Ali Imran for the pains he undertook and the enthusiasm with which he typed this manuscript.

UPENDRA CHOUDHURY

Abbreviations

ABM	Anti-Ballistic Missile
C^3	Command, Control, and Communication
CBM	Confidence Building Measure
CTBT	Comprehensive Test Ban Treaty
DAE	Department of Atomic Energy
DCC	Development Control Committee
DRDO	Defence Research and Development Organization
ECC	Employment Control Committee
IAEA	International Atomic Energy Agency
ICBM	Inter Continental Ballistic Missile
IRBM	Intermediate Range Ballistic Missile
IGMDP	Integrated Guided Missile Development Programme
ISI	Inter-Services Intelligence
NBC	Nuclear, Biological and Chemical
NEST	Nuclear Emergency Search Team
NFU	No-First-Use
NPT	Nuclear Non-Proliferation Treaty
NRRC	Nuclear Risk Reduction Centre
NRRMs	Nuclear Risk Reduction Measures
PAL	Permissive Action Link(s)
PRP	Personnel Reliability Programme
SLBM	Submarine Launched Ballistic Missile
SRBM	Short Range Ballistic Missile
WMD	Weapon(s) of Mass Destruction

Introduction

The last couple of years have brought significant changes in the relations between India and Pakistan. At the political level these include: the meeting of Prime Minister Atal Behari Vajpayee and President Pervez Musharraf in Islamabad in January 2004 and their readiness to revive the framework of contacts between India and Pakistan that was suspended following the crisis in 2001–2; the assumption of power by the Congress-led United Progressive Alliance (UPA) in May 2004 and its determination to continue the peace process initiated by the previous government; and the meeting between the new Indian Prime Minister Manmohan Singh and General Pervez Musharraf in New York in September 2004, in New Delhi in April 2005 and again in New York in September 2005. Changes at the nuclear level have also been notable as evidenced in the several rounds of Indo–Pakistani expert level talks on Nuclear Confidence Building Measures held since 2004. The joint statement released after the second meeting of Islamabad in 2004 reiterated their commitment 'to keep working towards elaboration and implementation of nuclear confidence building measures within the agreed framework of the Lahore MoU of 1999 and the Joint Statement of 20 June 2004'.

Despite these changes, however, the risk of intentional, accidental and unauthorized use of nuclear weapons remain a serious concern. Pakistan continues to stress on 'simultaneous' progress on all issues, especially Jammu & Kashmir, and the need for its final settlement within a 'reasonable time frame'. India perceives this Pakistani strategy as 'unfair' pressure tactics, tantamount to imposing preconditions on the ongoing composite dialogue. If the peace process is disrupted, Pakistan may again resume its policy of cross-border terrorism against India. This may force New Delhi to develop the necessary military options to deal with renewed terrorism from Islamabad. All this could lead to a state of very high tension between the two countries as in the past, raising nuclear risks in South Asia.

Although the India–Pakistan deterrent relationship is inherently unstable and poses immediate nuclear risks, security and stability in South Asia cannot be understood without taking into account the role of China. China is a key player in the region and affects its security in a number of ways. First, it has an ongoing border dispute with India. Second, it has supplied Weapons of Mass Destruction (WMD) technologies to Pakistan, perhaps to build it up as a military counterweight to India. Finally, its growing nuclear and missile muscle is seen as a serious concern by countries like India. Thus, since China is part of the problem in South Asia, its inclusion in any discussion is necessary for devising any credible nuclear solution for the subcontinent.

Study Approach

The prospect of a nuclear war between India and Pakistan has drawn global attention and concern. Should a nuclear exchange take place, no less than 12 million lives could be lost (US Department of Defense Report, 2002). It is in this context that this study assumes importance. It studies the nuclear relationship between India and Pakistan and between India and China since May 1998 and explores a wide range of measures by which these three countries could reduce nuclear risks in South Asia. It argues that improvements in bilateral relations and nuclear risk reduction are integrally linked and should not be viewed in isolation. Consequently, it recommends a phased approach to the problem. It suggests that in view of the prevailing suspicion, mistrust and animosity among these three countries, it would be best to concentrate first on measures that can be implemented without requiring any significant change in their current security policies. If these measures were implemented, they could lay the foundation for more significant measures at a later stage.

One of the difficulties in designing the necessary strategies and policies for reducing nuclear risks is the lack of Chinese willingness to enter into a nuclear dialogue with India. China even refuses to acknowledge India as a de facto nuclear weapon state. Hence, under the present circumstances, the best approach could be to negotiate bilateral risk reduction measures between India and Pakistan that do not compromise their national security. Once political problem solving and deepening economic cooperation begin to take root, India and China could start a nuclear dialogue and negotiate risk reduction measures either bilaterally or trilaterally (including Pakistan).

However, two points need special mention in this context. First, Nuclear Risk Reduction Measures (NRRMs) are valuable and necessary because they can raise the threshold of nuclear safety (making South Asia less unsafe). But they cannot eliminate nuclear risks from South Asia completely. In other words, even if NRRMs are negotiated and implemented in good faith, they cannot guarantee the non-use of nuclear weapons. For this, elimination of nuclear weapons through universal nuclear disarmament is needed. Second, India and Pakistan alone do not constitute South Asia. There are five other sovereign states that belong to the region, each with its own hopes and aspirations. But the use of nuclear weapons by either India or Pakistan would have impacts beyond the boundaries of these two countries and would threaten the survival of them all (Nepal, Bangladesh, Sri Lanka and Bhutan). Hence, the term South Asia has been used throughout the text.

CHAPTER 1

Understanding India's, Pakistan's and China's Nuclear Programmes

This chapter is divided into two parts. The first part summarizes the history of India's and Pakistan's nuclear programmes, their current nuclear and missile capabilities, command and control structures, nuclear doctrines, postures, targeting philosophies, and the impact of nuclear weapons use in South Asia. The second part discusses the Chinese nuclear forces, their use, and doctrines, among other things. Understanding these is necessary because they have a direct relationship with the unfolding crisis scenarios in the subcontinent. For instance, there is an organic link between Pakistan's first-strike nuclear posture and its support to cross-border terrorism in India. Besides, a familiarity with the Indian, Pakistani and Chinese nuclear doctrines and strategies will help us in suggesting various risk reduction measures that may be negotiated to bring nuclear stability in South Asia.

History of Nuclear Weapons Programmes of India and Pakistan

BACKGROUND

India

India's road to nuclear power status[1] began as early as 1948 with the establishment of the Atomic Energy Commission. Six years later, the Department of Atomic Energy was established. The

[1] For a comprehensive account of the origins of the Indian nuclear weapons programme, see George Perkovich, *India's Nuclear Bomb: The Impact on Global Proliferation*, Berkeley: University of California Press, 1999; and Government of

objective of the programme, at least until the 1962 Sino-Indian conflict, was to 'develop (atomic energy) for peaceful purposes'.[2]

After India's humiliating defeat in the 1962 border war with China, there was a demand for developing a nuclear bomb, which intensified after China's first nuclear test in 1964. Lal Bahadur Shastri, the then Indian prime minister failed in obtaining nuclear guarantees from the major power. He succumbed to their pressure and authorized a limited peaceful explosion programme, which could be converted into a military programme if the situat-ion so warranted.

India's strategic environment underwent a sea change after the 1971 war with Pakistan. The emergence of a US–China–Pakistan axis and President Nixon's dispatch of the USS Enterprise to the Bay of Bengal during the Bangladesh crisis provided the context for India's first nuclear test in 1974. Although Morarji Desai, who succeeded Indira Gandhi as prime minister, pledged 'not to manufacture or acquire nuclear weapons even if the rest of the world did so',[3] the programme was revived again under Indira Gandhi. Mrs Gandhi reportedly ordered a nuclear test in 1983, but changed her mind within the course of a day, perhaps due to the likely US reaction and its negative impact on India's economy. She, however, started India's Integrated Guided Missile Development Programme

---

India; 'The Evolution of India's Nuclear Policy', in *India's Nuclear Deterrent: Pokhran II and Beyond*, ed. Amitabh Mattoo, New Delhi: Har-Anand Publishers, 1998, Appendix II. For an account of Indian nuclear decision making, see Raj Chengappa, *Weapons of Peace: The Secret Story of India's Quest to Be a Nuclear Power*, New Delhi: HarperCollins, 2000. For an explanation of the motivation underlying India's decision to test nuclear weapons, see Sumit Ganguly, 'India's Pathway to Pokhran-II: The Sources and Prospects of India's Nuclear Weapons Programme', *International Security*, vol. 23, no. 4, Spring 1999, pp. 148–77; and Prem Shankar Jha, 'Why India Went Nuclear', *World Affairs*, vol. 2, no. 3, July–September 1998, pp. 80–96.

[2] Cited in Pratap Bhanu Mehta, 'India: The Nuclear Politics of Self-Esteem', *Current History*, vol. 97, no. 623, December 1998, p. 404.

[3] Cited in K. Subrahmanyam, 'India and the International Nuclear Order', in *Nuclear India in the Twenty-First Century*, ed. D. R. Sardesai and Raju Thomas, New York: Palgrave, 2002, p. 74.

(IGMDP) in 1983.[4] India tested its first short-range ballistic missile Prithvi in 1988, and the intermediate-range ballistic missile Agni in 1989.

According to the Kargil Review Committee Report, India's weaponization—the process of developing, testing and integrating components into a militarily deliverable warhead—took place between 1992 and 1994.[5] The decision to build a nuclear weapon occurred after two developments: Pakistan's success in the acquisition of uranium enrichment capacity and subsequently a weapons capability (as announced by A.Q. Khan in January 1987); and the Pakistan–China military cooperation based on a secret agreement in June 1976.

Two other international events in the second half of the 1990s accelerated India's nuclear weapons programme. The first was the permanent extension of the Nuclear Non-Proliferation Treaty (NPT) in 1995, and the second was the signing of the Comprehensive Test Ban Treaty (CTBT) in 1996.[6] The Bharatiya Janata Party (BJP), which was keen to make India a Nuclear Weapons State (NWS), came to power under the leadership of A.B. Vajpayee. Within just a month of assuming power, Vajpayee ordered five nuclear tests on 11 and 13 May 1998.

Thus, the nuclear weapons programme initiated by Indira Gandhi was continued by Rajiv Gandhi and fully operationalized by P.V. Narasimha Rao. The Janata Dal Prime Ministers V.P. Singh and Chandrashekhar and United Front Prime Ministers Deve Gowda and I.K. Gujral lent their full support to the programme.[7]

[4] For a comprehensive account of the origin of the IGMDP, see Upendra Choudhury, 'Security in a Period of Strategic Uncertainty: A Study of India's Ballistic Missile Programme', Ph.D. thesis, CPS/SSS, JNU, New Delhi, 1999.

[5] 'Nuclear Backdrop', *From Surprise to Reckoning: The Kargil Review Committee Report*, New Delhi: Sage, 2000, pp. 183–213.

[6] For a discussion on how NPT and CTBT influenced India's nuclear decision, see T.V. Paul, 'The Systemic Bases of India's Challenges to the World Nuclear Order', *Non-Proliferation Review*, vol. 6, no. 1, Fall 1998, pp. 1–11.

[7] K. Subrahmanyam, 'From Indira to Gowda: It was Bomb All the Way', *Times of India*, 17 April 2000.

In this sense, the BJP seems to have completed a programme for which previous governments had laid the groundwork.[8]

Pakistan

The Pakistani nuclear programme[9] started quite late with the establishment of the Atomic Energy Commission in 1957. However, following the Sino–Indian border war in 1962 and the Chinese nuclear test in 1964 when the debate for an 'Indian Bomb' pervaded Indian parliamentary and public life, Pakistan's then Foreign Minister, Z.A. Bhutto famously declared that if India developed an atomic bomb, Pakistan would follow.[10]

After Pakistan's humiliating defeat in the 1971 war with India, Prime Minister Bhutto made his famous 'we-will-eat-grass-but-we'll-have-our-bomb' speech in January 1972 at Multan in which he discussed making bombs with the Pakistani scientists.[11] Three years later, he put A.Q. Khan, a Pakistani metallurgist, in-charge of the country's nuclear weapons programme. Dr Khan, who had earlier worked at an enrichment plant in the Netherlands, made use of his Dutch connection to procure various sensitive material and equipment from European and North American sources.

[8] Most explanations of India's nuclear tests, specially the overt tests in May 1998, emphasize one or more factors: domestic politics, major-power ambition, international prestige, a desire to appease the nuclear scientific and technical enclave, etc. These may be some of the reasons, but they are not sufficient to explain India's nuclear tests. The May nuclear tests were the culmination of a process that began in the mid-1960s after a lot of parliamentary and public debate in India. Moreover, the BJP could hardly have demonstrated a nuclear testing programme barely seven weeks after coming to power had previous governments not prepared the way.

[9] For a detailed understanding of the history of Pakistan's nuclear weapons programme, see Shabidur Rehman, *Long Road to Chagai*, Islamabad: Print-Wise Publications, 1999. For a study of the factors that shaped Pakistan's decision to undertake nuclear explosions, see Hasan Askari Rizvi, 'Pakistan's Nuclear Testing', *Asian Survey*, vol. XLI, no. 6, November–December 2001, pp. 943–55; and Samina Yasmeen, 'Pakistan's Nuclear Tests: Domestic Debate and International Determinants', *Australian Journal of International Affairs*, vol. 53, no. 1, 1999, pp. 43–55.

[10] M.V. Ramana and A.H. Nayyar, 'India, Pakistan and the Bomb', *Scientific American*, December 2001, at: http://www.sciam.com/article.cfm?articleID=00087D79-AA4B-1C6E-84A9809EC588EF21&ref=sciam

[11] Subrahmanyam, op. cit., n. 3 above, p. 77.

Meanwhile, in June 1976, Pakistan concluded a secret agreement with China for collaboration in nuclear weapons technology. Thereafter, China played a very active role in helping build up Pakistan's nuclear and missile capabilities.[12] The Soviet invasion of Afghanistan made Pakistan a frontline state for the United States in its war against communism and immunized its nuclear weapons programme from international scrutiny.

In 1987, A.Q. Khan gave his famous interview to Indian journalist Kuldip Nayar when he publicly declared that Pakistan had the bomb, or, to be more precise, could assemble it immediately if required. Pakistan's nuclear weapons capability was again confirmed in 1990 when the US president was unable to certify to the US Congress as per the Pressler Amendment[13] that Pakistan did not possess a nuclear explosive device. Meanwhile, in the early 1990s, Pakistan was developing its weapons delivery capability by procuring various missile systems, initially from China, and later from North Korea. It test-fired its first ballistic missile, Hatf-I, in 1989 and the first Intermediate Range Ballistic Missile (IRBM), Ghauri, in April 1998.[14]

The final Pakistani decision to openly enter the nuclear weapons club came in May 1998 after India conducted five nuclear tests the same month. Prime Minister Nawaz Sharif authorized the detonation of six nuclear devices on 28 and 30 May, apparently to establish parity with India by taking into account the latter's 1974 explosion of a 'peaceful nuclear test'.

[12] For a discussion on China's role in Pakistan's nuclear and missile programme, see Mohan Malik, 'Nuclear Proliferation in Asia: The China Factor', *Australian Journal of International Affairs*, vol. 53, no. 1, 1999, pp. 31–41; and T.V Paul, 'Chinese–Pakistani Missile Ties and the Balance of Power', *Non-Proliferation Review*, vol. 10, no. 2, Summer 2003, pp. 1–9.

[13] In 1985, US Senator Larry Pressler introduced what is known as the Pressler Amendment, which required the US president to certify annually to Congress that Pakistan 'does not possess a nuclear explosive device and that the proposed US assistance programme will reduce significantly the risk that Pakistan will possess a nuclear explosive device'.

[14] For a detailed account of the history of Pakistan's ballistic missile programme, see Upendra Choudhury, 'Ballistic Missiles and India–Pakistan Strategic Balance', *Journal of Peace Studies*, vol. 9, no. 5, September–October 2002, pp. 52–5.

Nuclear Capabilities

The sizes and details of India's and Pakistan's current nuclear forces are not certain, but various estimates provide a reasonable picture.

India

Jane's, the military analysis group based in London, estimates that India has between 50 and 150 nuclear warheads.[15] The Institute for Science and International Security (ISIS) in Washington says India has about 65 warheads.[16] The Stockholm International Peace Research Institute (SIPRI) estimates that India has between 25 and 40 warheads.[17] *BAS*, a Chicago-based bimonthly on global security news and analysis and published by the Educational Foundation for Nuclear Scinece estimates that India has a stockpile of approximately 30–5 nuclear warheads (fewer than Pakistan).[18] The Natural Resources Defence Council (NRDC), New York, estimates that India has enough material for up to 50 warheads.[19] In 1999, the Congressional Research Service—the public policy research arm of the US Congress, Washington D.C put the number at 75 or more.[20]

[15] For an overview of Jane's survey of India's nuclear weapons capability, see 'Indian Nuke Arsenal Dwarfs Pak', *Times of India*, 1 June 2002.

[16] For more, see David Albright, 'India's and Pakistan's Fissile Material and Nuclear Weapons Inventories, End of 1999', The Institute for Science and International Security, Washington, Oct. 2000, at: http://www.isisonline.org/publications/SouthAsia/stocks/000.html

[17] Cited in Robin Rowland, 'Nuclear Nightmare in South Asia: FAQs', CBC News Online, 31 May 2002, at: http://www.cbc.ca/news/background/india_pakistan/nuclear_faq.html

[18] 'India's Nuclear Forces, 2002', *Bulletin of Atomic Scientists* report available at: http://www.thebulletin.org/issues/nukenotes/ma02nukenote.html

[19] Rowland, op. cit., n. 17 above.

[20] CRS report cited in Hilary Synnott, *The Causes and Consequences of South Asia's Nuclear Tests*, Adelphi Paper 332, London: International Institute for Strategic Studies, London, 1999, p. 55.

Pakistan

According to Jane's, Pakistan has between 25 and 50 warheads.[21] The ISIS says Pakistan has about 40 warheads,[22] SIPRI estimates Pakistan as having between 15 and 20 warheads,[23] the Congressional Research Service estimates between 10 and 15 weapons,[24] and NRDC suggests that Pakistan has sufficient material to arm a dozen weapons.[25] According to BAS, Pakistan has between 24 and 48 nuclear weapons.[26]

Similarly, on the basis of their claims of the May 1998 nuclear tests, it is believed that both India and Pakistan are capable of producing a relatively wide range of nuclear warheads.[27] However, independent seismic analysts suggest that the actual yields were lower than the official pronouncements.[28]

However, three things need special mention here. First, India has, and probably will retain, a significant lead over Pakistan in

[21] Jane's, op. cit., n. 15 above.

[22] Albright, op. cit., n. 16 above.

[23] Rowland, op. cit., n. 17 above.

[24] Synnott, op. cit., n. 20 above.

[25] 'Pakistan's Nuclear Forces, 2002', *Bulletin of Atomic Scientists* report available at: http://www.thebulletin.org/issues/nukenotes/jf02nukenote.html

[26] 'Pakistan's Nuclear Forces, 2001', in NRDC Nuclear Notebook, *Bulletin of Atomic Scientists*, 7 June 2002, at: http://www.thebulletin.org/issues/nukenotes/jf02nukenote.html

[27] For a summary of critiques of the possible yields of the nuclear weapons, see Praful Bidwai and Achin Vanaik, *South Asia on a Short-Fuse: Nuclear Politics and the Future of Global Disarmament*, New Delhi: Oxford University Press, 1999. Also see the debate 'The Question of Nuclear Yield: BAARC Scientists Present Proof', *Frontline*, vol. 16, no. 25, 27 November–10 December 1999, at: http://www.frontlineonnet.com/fl1625/16250810.htm

[28] According to the Government of India, the three devices that were tested on 11 May 1998 at the Pokhran test site included a fission device, with an yield of about 12 KT, a thermonuclear device with an yield of 43 KT, and a low-yield sub-kiloton device. On 13 May 1998, India conducted two further tests, which were also low-yield devices in the sub-kiloton range. Pakistan had similarly claimed on 31 May that all of its six tests had involved boosted fission devices using Uranium 235. The cumulative yields were 50 KT, comprising one detonation of 25 KT, two of 12 KT, and three with sub-kiloton yields.

strategic nuclear forces,[29] but these are fewer than China's estimated arsenal of about 450 weapons.[30] Second, while the size and shape of their current nuclear capabilities can be debated, there is no disagreement that both India and Pakistan have produced and tested weapons with sufficient yields to provide for significant destruction. Even at the lowest estimates, both sides also have sufficient numbers of weapons to do tremendous damage in a nuclear exchange. Finally, most assessments say that both India and Pakistan are slowly but steadily increasing their nuclear stockpiles.

Delivery Systems

Both India and Pakistan have different types of aircraft and nuclear capable missiles that could be used as delivery vehicles for nuclear weapons.

Aircraft

India: India has four different types of nuclear capable strike aircraft: the British Jaguar low-level strike aircraft, the French multi-role Mirage-2000 fighter jets, the old Soviet MiG-29 fighters, and the new Russian multi-variant SU-30 fighter-bomber. While the SU-30s, MiG-29s and Mirage-2000s are designed primarily for air-superiority missions, they could also be converted to serve effectively as nuclear delivery platforms.[31] However, the uncertainties over their penetration capabilities and survivability of fighter aircraft after a pre-emptive strike have already forced India to shift its force structure towards land-based ballistic missiles.

[29] An ABC TV report on 7 June 2000, ostensibly based on information leaked by a US intelligence agency, stated that Pakistan had 25 to 100 nuclear weapons, 'five times' India's arsenal. It also gave Pakistan a major lead in ballistic missile capability based on Chinese and North Korean designs and claimed that India was trailing way behind. However, Pakistan formally denied the assessment: Ramesh Chandran, 'Pak N-Might Bigger than India's, Says US', *Times of India*, 8 June 2000.

[30] 'China's Nuclear Forces, 2003, *Bulletin of Atomic Scientists* report available at: http://www.thebulletin.org/issues/nukenotes/jf02nukenote.html

[31] For more, see Paul Jackson, ed., *Jane's All the World's Aircraft 2002–2003*, Coulson, UK: Jane's Information Group, 2002, pp. 114–18, 405–6.

Pakistan: Pakistani aircraft which could be used for dropping nuclear weapons include A-5 Fantans, the French Mirage-III/5s, and American F-16s. However, their limited combat ranges, penetrability concerns, and vulnerability to first-strikes have relegated these fighters to last-resort missions.[32] Moreover, the availability of ballistic missiles has also reduced the relevance of aircraft as delivery vehicles for nuclear weapons.

Missiles

India: In addition to nuclear capable aircraft, India has the short-range Prithvi and medium-range Agni missiles for delivering nuclear weapons. Between these delivery systems, most of mainland China and all of Pakistan are covered.[33] The details of Indian nuclear capable missiles are given in Table 1.1.

TABLE 1.1 INDIA'S BALLISTIC MISSILES

	Range (*km*)	Payload (*kg*)	Comments
Prithvi I	150	1,000	Deployed
Prithvi II	250	500	Undergoing user trials
Prithvi III or Dhanush	250	500	Ship-launched versio nunder development
Agni	1,000-1,500	1,000	Shelved in favour ofAgni II
Agni I	700-800	1,000	Fills gap between short-range and intermediate-range missiles
Agni II	2,000-2,500	1,000	Tested to a range of more than 2,000 km
Agni III	3,500-4,000	1,000	Under development

India is also working on a nuclear submarine project code-named Advanced Technology Vessel (ATV). This project, which

[32] Upendra Choudhury, 'Too Close for Comfort', *Bulletin of Atomic Scientists*, vol. 59, no. 2, March–April 2003, pp. 22–5.

[33] Praveen Swami, 'Nuclear Submarine Project May Get a Kick-Start', *Hindu*, 27 May 2004. Also see Andrew Koch, 'Nuclear Power Submarine: India's Strategic Trump Card', *Jane's Intelligence Review*, vol. 59, no. 2, June 1998, pp. 29–31.

TABLE 1.2 PAKISTAN'S BALLISTIC MISSILES

	Range (*km*)	Payload (*kg*)	Comments
Hatf-II or Abdali	180	500	30+ stored at airbase near Lahore
Hatf-III or Ghaznavi	290	500	Reportedly based on China's M-11
Hatf-IV or Shaheen-I	750	700	Reportedly based on China's M-9
Hatf-VI or Shaheen-II	750	1,000	Under development?
Hatf-V or Ghauri	2,000	700	Based on North Korean Nodong; tested to 1,100 km
Ghauri II	1,200-1,500	700	Tested to 1,165 km

was initiated in 1976 and based on a Charlie-I class Soviet submarine, is scheduled for completion in 2008–9.[34]

Pakistan: Pakistan has Hatf, Ghauri and Shaheen missiles that cover most of the Indian mainland (Table 1.2).

Presently, sea-based nuclear capabilities belong in the theoretical realm for Pakistan. However, according to a report, the Pakistan Navy signed a deal with France in September 1994 for the purchase of three Agosta 90B submarines, which could be used as platforms to launch ballistic missiles with nuclear warheads.[35]

Nuclear Use Doctrines

The nuclear doctrines of India and Pakistan governing the use of nuclear weapons in the case of a conflict are discussed below.

[34] For more, see Andrew C. Winner and Toshi Yoshihara, *Nuclear Stability in South Asia*, Institute for Foreign Policy Analysis, Spring 2002, at: http://www.ifpa.org/pdf/nssa.pdf

[35] Abdul Hameed Toor, 'Technology and Operational Capabilities of Agosta 90B Submarine', paper presented at the 15th Summer Symposium on Science and World Affairs, 23–31 July 2003, Moscow, p. 1.

India

India has declared a No-First-Use (NFU) nuclear doctrine,[36] which has the following characteristics. First, India will use its nuclear weapons in 'retaliation only' to inflict unacceptable damage to the enemy. Second, it will not use nuclear weapons against non-NWS. Third, in the event of a major attack against India or Indian forces anywhere by biological or chemical weapons, India will retain the option of retaliating with nuclear weapons. And finally, India is committed to building a minimum credible deterrent, which implies that India's nuclear policy, strategy and posture will be guided by a 'minimalist principle'. Although Indian defence analysts seem to be divided over what constitutes a 'minimum nuclear deterrent', most of them are of the view that India will, in any case, take its own time in determining the minimum depending on its assessment of threats, its capabilities, and, presumably, the economic costs involved.[37]

Pakistan

Pakistan has not publicly announced a nuclear doctrine as India has, but two basic elements of its nuclear policy can be gleaned from statements made by the country's top leaders and high-level government officials: keeping a 'nuclear first-use option', and resorting to early use in case of even a conventional war. Conventional military inferiority vis-à-vis India and lack of strate-

[36] For more on India's nuclear doctrine, see 'India Spells Draft Nuclear Doctrine', *Hindustan Times*, 18 August 1999, India's Draft Nuclear Doctrine report of the National Security Advisory Board, 17 Aug. 1999, at: http://www.indianembassy.org/policy/CTBT/nuclear_doctrine_aug_17_1999.html; W. P. S. Sidhu, 'India's Nuclear Use Doctrine' in *Planning the Unthinkable: How New Powers Will Use Nuclear Biological and Chemical Weapons*, ed. Peter R. Levoy, S. D. Sagan and J. J. Wirtz, Ithaca: Cornell University Press, 2000; and Gurmeet Kanwal, 'India's Nuclear Doctrine and Policy', *Strategic Analysis*, vol. xxiv, no. 11, February 2001 pp. 1951–72.

[37] For more on this aspect, see Kanti Bajpai, 'India's Nuclear Posture After Pokhran II', International Studies, vol. 37, no. 4, October–December 2000, pp. 61–108.

gic depth are said to be the reasons for this nuclear policy of Pakistan.[38]

Nuclear Postures

India

India has adopted what Ashley Tellis calls a 'distributed nuclear posture'.[39] Such a posture implies that under normal circumstances, India's nuclear components are deliberately kept separated. This separation of components has been further complemented by vesting authority and responsbility on a organization basis: the Department of Atomic Energy (DAE) and the Defence Research and Development Organization (DRDO), both civilian agencies, retain the custody of the fissile core and weapons assembly (either jointly or separately), while the nuclear capable delivery systems remain in the custody of the military.

Pakistan

Pakistan, like India, is believed to have kept its nuclear weapons in a 'disassembled state', meaning probably that the fission core is kept separately from the non-nuclear (ignition) components. Nevertheless, according to General Khalid Kidwai of the Strategic Plans Division, the bombs can be assembled 'very quickly'.[40]

[38] For more on Pakistan's nuclear doctrine, see Zafar Iqbal Cheema, 'Pakistan's Nuclear Use Doctrine and Command and Control', in Levoy et al., op. cit., n. 36 above. Also see Saeed Ismat, 'Strategy for Total Defence: A Conceptual Nuclear Doctrine', *Pakistan Defence Journal,* March 2000, at: http://www.defencejournal.com/2000/mar/doctrine.htm

[39] Ashley J. Tellis, 'Towards a Force-in-Being: The Logic, Structure and Utility of India's Emerging Nuclear Posture', *Strategic Studies* (special issue), India as an *Emerging Power,* vol. 25, no. 4, 2003, p. 84.

[40] General Kidwai, quoted in Paolo Cotta-Ramusino and Maurizio Martellini, 'Nuclear Safety, Nuclear Stability and Nuclear Strategy in Pakistan', a concise report of a visit by Landau Network-Centro-Volta, 21 January 2002, at: http://axmi.mi.infn.it/~landnet/Doc/pakistan.pdf

COMMAND AND CONTROL STRUCTURES

This is the link between the National Command Authority (NCA), the decision makers who ultimately control the release of the nuclear weapons, and the personnel who have physical control of the weapons.

India

To manage and control its nuclear weapons, India established the NCA in January 2003. The NCA comprises a Political Council (PC) and an Executive Council (EC). The Political Council is chaired by the Prime Minister and 'is the sole body that can authorize the use of nuclear weapons'.[41] The Executive Council is chaired by the National Security Adviser to the Prime Minister and 'provides inputs for decision making by the NCA and executes the directives given to it by the Political Council'.[42] One rung below the Executive Council is the Strategic Forces Command that is headed by a Commander-in-Chief. The command is a mixed one, with representation from the three military services and will exercise overall operational control for the nuclear forces.

Pakistan

Pakistan set up an NCA in February 2000, which is responsible for policy formulation and 'exercise employment and development control over all strategic nuclear forces and organizations'.[43] It comprises two committees, the Employment Control Committee (ECC) and Development Control Committee (DCC), both

[41] C. Raja Mohan, 'Nuclear Command System Credible: India', *Hindu*, 8 January 2003.

[42] Ibid.

[43] 'National Command Authority Established', Associated Press of Pakistan, 3 February 2000, available at: http://www.fas.org/news/pakistan/2000/000203-pak-appl.htm; also see Zafer Nawaz Jaspal, 'Safety and Security of Pakistan's Nuclear Capabilities', *IPRI Journal*, vol. 2, no. 1, Winter 2002, at: http://www.ipri-pak-org/winterjournal02/safetyandsecurity.htm; and Shaun Gregory, 'A Formidable Challenge: Nuclear Command and Control in South Asia', Disarmament Diplomacy, no. 54, February 2001, at: http://www.acronym.org.uk/dd/dd54/54greg.htm

chaired by the Head of the Government. The ECC develops policy for the deployment and use of nuclear weapons and includes several civilians among its members. The DCC, in which only military officers presently serve, guides the design and evolution of Pakistan's nuclear capabilities. The Strategic Plans Division, headed by a three-star general, functions as the secretariat for the NCA and performs the functions of planning and coordination. A Strategic Forces Command has also been created.

Targeting Philosophies

In nuclear parlance, targets are divided into two categories: *counter-force*, which are essentially an enemy's military targets such as missile silos (the hardened shelters for ballistic missiles capable of withstanding a nuclear attack) nuclear airfields, bases, installations, etc., and *counter-value*, that involves striking the nation's population and industrial installations.

India

India's minimum deterrence nuclear policy and declared no-first-use 'punitive retaliation' doctrine appears to suggest retaliation mainly against the large population and industrial centres of its adversaries to obtain maximum pay-offs with its small nuclear force. In Pakistan's case, India could target three major urban areas such as Islamabad, Lahore and Karachi to inflict unacceptable and devastating damage.[44]

Pakistan

Pakistan, with its smaller nuclear forces, may target India's industrial and population centres, especially New Delhi (to wipe out India's political leadership) and Mumbai (the commercial hub). As Amitabh Mattoo says, 'Such a massive strike rests on Pakistan's hope that it would leave India shell-shocked and given its level of efficiency, cripple its capacity to strike back. There is also the

[44] For more, see Gurmeet Kanwal, 'Nuclear Targeting Philosophy for India', *Strategic Analysis*, vol. xxiv, no. 3, June 2000, pp. 459–74; and M.R. Srinivasan, 'Indo-Pak Nuclear Asymmetry', *Hindu*, 1 August 2001.

hope that the international community would take charge and prevent an Indian retaliation.'[45] Pakistan's rejection of the Indian proposal to extend the 1988 agreement to industrial and population centres clearly proves that Pakistan is retaining the option of counter-value strikes. It is, however, worthy of mention that a counter-force and a counter-value distinction are irrelevant in the Indo-Pakistani context because of geographical proximity and the large population density of the two countries.

Impact of Nuclear Weapons Use

An analysis of a nuclear war between India and Pakistan conducted by the US Department of Defense and leaked to the *New York Times* estimates that about 12 million people could be killed immediately in a nuclear exchange and as many as another 7 million injured. The Defense Department noted that these figures 'were just immediate casualties and more would die in the resulting fire storms in cities and even more as a result of disease and starvation'.[46] According to the *New Scientist*, a more limited attack could kill about 3 million people and injure 1.5 million.[47] M.V. Ramana and his colleagues of the Princeton University's Programme for Science and Global Security estimate that close to 3 million people in both countries would die in such an attack. Another 1.5 million people could be severely injured.[48] Most of

[45] Amitabh Mattoo, quoted in Raj Chengappa, 'If Pakistan Nukes India', *India Today*, 10 June 2002, pp. 24–32.

[46] US Department of Defense report summarized in 'Nuclear War Will Claim 12 Million Lives', *Hindu*, 28 May 2002.

[47] Ibid.

[48] For more, see M.V. Ramana, *Bombing Bombay: Effects of Nuclear Weapons and a Case Study of a Hypothetical Explosion*, Cambridge: International Physicians for the Prevention of Nuclear War, 1999. Several other reports are there on the impact of nuclear weapons in South Asia. See, for instance, S. Rashid Naim, '*Aadhi Raat Ke Baad*' (After Midnight), in *Nuclear Proliferation in South Asia: The Prospects for Arms Control*, ed. Stephen Philip Cohen, Boulder, CO: Westview Press, 1999; Chengappa, op. cit., n. 45 above; Priya Nayar, 'Face Off: A Nuclear Gamble', *Hindu*, 24 May 2003; NRDC's report on the consequences of nuclear conflict between India and Pakistan at: http://www.nrdc.org/nuclear/southasia.asp; Mathew McKinzi, Zia Mian, M.V. Ramana and A.H. Nayyar, *Nuclear War in South Asia*, FPIF Policy Report, June 2002.

these estimates are based on studies of the impact of the nuclear strikes on Hiroshima and Nagasaki in 1945.[49]

China's Nuclear Forces and Capability

While it is very difficult to get any accurate data on nuclear weapons and stockpiles in open democracies, getting such information about a totalitarian country like China is close to impossible. Yet, odd statements from Chinese sources and open literature from other countries give some clues in this regard. China exploded its first nuclear device in 1964 and its first thermonuclear device

TABLE 1.3 CHINESE NUCLEAR FORCES: JANUARY 1999

Type	NATO Designation	Range (km)	Warheads/ Yield	Warheads in Stockpiles
Aircraft				
H-6	B-6	3,100	1–3 bombs	120
Q-5	A-5	400	1 bomb	30
Land-based missiles				
DF-3A	CSS-2	2,800	1/3.3 MT	40
DF-4	CSS-3	4,750	1/3.3 MT	20
DF-5A	CSS-4	13,000	1/4.5 MT	20
DF-21A	CSS-6	1,800	1/200-300 KT	48
SLBMs				
Julang-1	CSS-N-3	1,700	1/200-30 KT	12
Julang-2	CSS-N-4	8,000	1/200-300 KT	?
Tactical weapons				
Artillery/ ADMs	Short-range missiles	1,000	Low KT	120

Source: *SIPRI Yearbook 1999*, Armament, Disarmament and International Security, OUP, 1999, p. 555.

[49] The US dropped a 15 KT nuclear warhead on Hiroshima and a 21 KT device on Nagasaki. The blast killed half of Hiroshima's 370,000 residents. In Nagasaki, one-fourth of the people died. In all, 300,000 people died and an equal number suffered serious injuries.

in 1967. It has conducted a total of 45 nuclear tests, and has about 450 nuclear warheads (300 strategic and 150 tactical warheads).[50] This makes it the third-largest nuclear power in the world. It is also reported that China's stockpile has more than 3 tonnes of weapons grade, highly enriched uranium and 1 tonne of separated plutonium with which it can make an additional 200 nuclear weapons.[51]

The Chinese Air Force has Q-5 and H-6 bombers. Between these, the latter can reach all Asian countries within a flying range of 3,100 km, but its capability to penetrate air defence systems is poor.[52] According to reports, China is also developing its first supersonic and only modern bomber, the H-7.[53] This all-weather bomber will be capable of carrying out nuclear missions for the Chinese Air Force and Navy. There are also reports that Russia has delivered about 80 of the two-seater Su-30 Mk2 fighter-bomber to China and in early 2003 Beijing signed a contract with Moscow for the delivery of Su-30 upgrades, the Su-30 Mk2 and Su-30 Mk3.[54]

China has a variety of land-based missiles including more than a dozen Inter Continental Ballistic Missile (ICBM). Its short-, intermediate-, medium- and long-range missiles are, however, more relevant to South Asia. The DF-11, DF-15 and the CSS-8 are the three Short Range Ballistic Missile (SRBM). The DF-11 has a range of 1,000 km. The DF-15 bears the export designation of M-9, while the CSS-8 is exported (to Iran) as the M-7. The IRBM class of missiles include the DF-3A with a range of 2,800 km and the DF-4 with a range of 4,750 km. The DF-21A is an

[50] Ming Zhang, 'Summary of China's Nuclear Weapons and Policies', Appendix C, in *China's Changing Nuclear Posture: Reactions to the South Asian Nuclear Tests*, Washington, DC: Carnegie Endowment for International Peace Paper, 1999, at: http://www.ceip.org/pubs/china-zhang/CH2.PDF

[51] Lisbeth Gronlund, David Wright and Yong Liu, 'China and a Fissile Material Production Cut-Off', *Survival*, vol. 37, no. 4, Winter 1995–6, pp. 150–1.

[52] Zhang, op. cit., n. 50 above, p. 2.

[53] Ibid.

[54] Richard D. Fisher, 'China Accelerates Navy Building', *China Brief*, vol. III, issue 15, 29 July 2003, p. 10

Medium Range Ballistic Missiles (MRBM) with a range of 1,800 km. Although this missile is nuclear capable, it is being modified for a conventional role, indicating how the Chinese perceive missiles as war-fighting weapons.[55] There are reports that China is improving the number and accuracy of its medium- and short-range missiles and using global-positioning satellite systems to improve their accuracy.[56]

Chinese Submarine Launched Ballistic Missiles (SLBM) include the JL-1 and JL-2 with ranges of 1,700 and 8,000 km respectively. Although China has a small number of ICBMs (about 20), they represent the Chinese desire to possess a nuclear deterrent that is global in reach. Analysts believe that they are designed to provide an overall shield of nuclear deterrence under which a conventional local/limited war can be fought without being subjected to nuclear blackmail.[57]

China stores its nuclear warheads separately from its missiles.[58] These missiles are widely dispersed to ensure that they are not destroyed in a concerted attack. Some of them are reportedly deployed in caves in the mountains.[59]

China operates a single Xia-class nuclear submarine that carries 12 single-warhead Julang-1 ballistic missiles with an estimated range of 1,700 km.[60] The Xia's missile system is not fully operational, however. The CIA and the Pentagon characterize J-1 missiles as 'experimental'. China has also begun work on a new

[55] A.K. Sachdev, 'Chinese Missiles: Winning the Limited War', *Strategic Analysis*, vol. xxiv, no. 3, June 2000, p. 532.

[56] Avery Goldstein, 'Great Expectations: Interpreting China's Arrival', *International Security*, vol. 22, no. 3, Winter 1997/8, p. 49.

[57] Sachdev, op. cit., n. 55 above, p. 533.

[58] Robert E. Rehbein, 'Managing Proliferation in South Asia: A Case for Assistance to Unsafe Nuclear Arsenals', *Non-Proliferation Review*, vol. 9, no. 1, Spring 2002, p. 97.

[59] Dan Caldwell, 'PLAs: A Description and Proposal', *Survival*, May–June 1987, pp. 224–38.

[60] Robert S. Norris and Hans M. Kristensen, 'Chinese Nuclear Forces, 2003', *Bulletin of the Atomic Scientists*, vol. 59, no. 6, November–December 2003, pp. 77–80, at: http://www.thebulletin.org/article_nn.php?art_ofn=nd03norris

SLBM called Project-094. This submarine is expected to carry 16 three-stage Julang-2 ballistic missiles, a variant of the DF-31 missile, with an estimated range of up to 8,000 km.[61] Given the significant problems China has had with the Xia, the deployment of the Project 094 submarine is many years away.

The State Council in China directs and administers national defence, and the Central Military Commission (with the state President as its Chairman) commands the nation's armed forces, including the nuclear forces.[62] The CMC also plays a role in Chinese nuclear release procedures.[63]

China has officially declared an NFU nuclear policy and no-use or threat-of-using nuclear weapons against non-NWS or zones. However, in recent years, there has been a perceptible change in the Chinese military doctrine.[64] In early 1998, the People's Liberation Army (PLA) conducted a round of exercises whose purpose, according to Chinese officials, was to prepare the country's forces to win a regional war using of high-tech weapons.[65]

[61] Ibid.

[62] Information Office of the State Council, People's Republic of China, 'China's National Defense' at: htpp://www.chinaembassy.org/Cgi-Bin/Press.pl?wparms. Zhang points out that the Standing Committee of the Political Bureau of the Chinese Communist Party still has the final say on all major security policies.

[63] Scila McLean, ed., *China: How Nuclear Decisions are Made*, New York: St. Martin's Press, 1986, pp. 186–203. Also see 'PRC, Nuclear Weapons Employment Policy and Strategy', Annex C, Command and Control, at: http://www.fas.org/irp/dia/product/prc_72/app_c.htm

[64] Swaran Singh, 'China's Nuclear Weapons and Doctrine', in *Nuclear India*, ed. Jasjit Singh, New Delhi: Knowledge World, in association with IDSA (Institute of Defence Studies and Analyses), 1998, p. 152.

[65] http://www.ceip.org/pubs/china-zhang/CH4.PDF Zhang, op. cit., Ch. 4, p. 36.

CHAPTER 2

Nuclear Risks in South Asia

After a brief overview of the Indian, Pakistani and Chinese nuclear programmes, it would be pertinent to discuss the nature and kinds of nuclear risks prevalent in South Asia. But before doing that, it is important to understand the two dominant nuclear narratives prevailing in this region. The first is between those who consider South Asia as a 'nuclear flashpoint' and those who reject this assumption. The second relates to the assumption that rivalry between India and Pakistan is South Asia's primary determinant of security and stability. It is necessary to discuss these two narratives in detail, and only then it will be possible for us to design policies for nuclear risk reduction that have a lasting impact on the subcontinent.

South Asia as a Nuclear Flashpoint: Myth and Reality

Following the tit-for-tat nuclear tests by India and Pakistan, South Asia has been described as a potential nuclear flashpoint. This has become an article of faith among many Western countries, espec-

[1] For instance, former US President Bill Clinton referred to the Indian subcontinent as one of Asia's 'most dangerous flash-points': see Ramesh Chandran, 'Clinton Finds LoC Most Dangerous Place in World', *Times of India*, 17 March 2000. Similarly, US Director of the CIA George Tenet testified to the US Congress in early 2001 that 'relations between India and Pakistan remain volatile making the risk of war between the two nuclear armed adversaries unacceptably high'. See his statement at: http://www.odci.gov/public_affairs/speeches/UNCLASSWWT_020/2001.html. For more, see Raju Thomas, 'Whither Nuclear India?', in *Nuclear India in the Twenty-First Century*, ed. D.R. Sardesai and Raju Thomas, New York: Palgrave, 2002, pp. 10–11; Paul D. Taylor, 'Nuclear War Between India and Pakistan is a Real Possibility?', *International Herald Tribune*, 16 March 2000; 'The World's Most Dangerous Place', *Economist*, 16 March 2000, p. 17.

ially American politicians, officials, academics and commentators.[1] There are, several reasons for this. First, recurring India–Pakistan military crises during 1986–7, 1990, and 1999 and in 2001–2 have resulted in such a perception. Second, the shrill rhetoric and tit-for-tat missile tests during crises have tended to add to this belief.

Several scholars, policy makers, government officials and analysts in the region (many in India and few from Pakistan) have, however, rejected this Western flashpoint theory by terming it alarmist and unrealistic. They argue that Indo-Pakistani relations are actually quite stable and the chances of nuclear weapons use or large-scale war between them is quite low.[2] They particularly emphasize the uniquely stabilizing elements of the Indo-Pakistani nuclear relationship, especially Indian No-First-Use (NFU), delayed strike, the non-centrality of nuclear weapons in national security strategy, the Indo-Pakistani non-alert nuclear deployment policy that the weapons should never be put in a state of instant readiness for use, as strong evidence in favour of their explanation.

For them, such Western discussion and analysis have a condescending and colonial tone, implying that 'the subcontinent is full of unstable people with deep historical resentments, incapable of acting rationally or managing a technologically sophisticated arsenal'.[3] Moreover, in these analyses, they find a need for outside involvement being projected, which India has resisted (particularly

[2] Three prominent analysts who advocate this viewpoint include: Jasjit Singh, 'Nuclear Command and Control', *Strategic Analysis*, vol. XXV, no. 2, May 2001, pp. 147-59; Ashley Tellis, *India's Emerging Nuclear Posture: Between Recessed Deterrent and Ready Arsenal*, Santa Monica: Rand, 2001; and K. Subrahmanyam, 'Nuclear India in Global Politics', *Strategic Digest*, vol. XXVIII, no. 12, December 1998, pp. 2003–18.

[3] Pratap Bhanu Mehta, 'India: The Nuclear Politics of Self-Esteem', *Current History*, vol. 97, no. 623, December 1998, p. 405. Former Indian Defence Minister George Fernandes similarly asserted that any doubt cast from outside over the ability of India and Pakistan to handle their nuclear responsibilities are rooted in double standards and even racism. The underlying belief (of our Western critics) is that 'Bombs are safe in our hands. But after they cross [the] Arabian Sea and move eastward, they are not': cited in 'India and Pakistan Camped on Brink of War Over Kashmir', News Review, *Disarmament Diplomacy*, no. 65, July–August 2002, at: http://www.acronym.org.uk/dd/dd65/65nr01.htm

regarding the Kashmir issue) as being ploys to pressurize New Delhi on the issue of non-proliferation.[4]

This either-or depiction of the subcontinent's nuclear situation is misleading for several reasons. Those who describe South Asia as a nuclear flashpoint should realize that nuclear weapons are destabilizing even in the arsenals of the 'old' nuclear powers. Similarly, those who brush aside the nuclear risks in the subcontinent should remember that the stabilizing elements of the South Asian nuclear balance are valid as long as there is no 'war' or 'warlike situation' in the subcontinent. Once war begins or crisis escalates to a warlike situation, several nuclear risks will come into being.

An Indo-Pakistani Rivalry Framework for South Asia?

Clearly related to the first is the assumption that the rivalry between India and Pakistan is South Asia's primary determinant of security and stability. This assumption is inadequate for two reasons. First, it underplays the strategic concerns and significance of India by positing equality between India and Pakistan. Second, it frames security and stability in South Asia only in terms of the Indo-Pakistani conflict. But this security is affected by extra-regional actors as well, specially China.

Undoubtedly, India is a major power in the making. The under-appreciation or underestimation of India by positing it as an equal of Pakistan is an unrealistic proposition that does not tally with the ground realities in the subcontinent. India outstrips Pakistan by any measure of power–territory, population, size of economy, scientific and technological know-how, political institutions. . . .[5]

Similarly, as discussed earlier, while national security and equality with India are the two key considerations underlying Pakistan's nuclear programme, India's move to acquire nuclear weapons

[4] For instance, see K. K. Katyal, 'Talk of Nuclear Conflict Again', *Hindu*, 19 April 2001; and Jasjit Singh, 'War in Slow Motion', *Indian Express*, 27 May 2003.

[5] Muthiah Alagappa, 'Nuclear Tests in South Asia', *Hindu*, 13 July 1998.

capability is primarily to counter what it perceives to be the intimidating nuclear might of China. Whether it is the humiliating defeat of India in the 1962 border war with China or the Chinese nuclear test in 1964, Beijing's nuclear and missile assistance to Islamabad or its threat to use tactical nuclear arms against India in the 1986–7 border skirmishes, the China factor has always influenced Indian security planning and shaped India's attitudes on international non-proliferation controls (discussed later in this chapter).[6] However, it cannot be denied that Islamabad's nuclear drive has prompted New Delhi to accelerate work on its nuclear programme.

Therefore, any frameworks for risk reduction in South Asia must not only acknowledge the strategic significance of India—which is only likely to increase—but also take into account the role of China.

The recognition of the China factor in the South Asian security matrix does not mean that the India-China nuclear relationship poses the same type of nuclear risks as does the India–Pakistan nuclear dyad. This is because the general tenor and trend of the two are very different. For instance, despite the persistence of sources of tension, India and China have so far managed their relationship relatively well. It appears that they have reached an understanding that their persistent differences on the border issue, nuclear issue and on the nature of the Chinese–Pakistani relationship should not be allowed to prevent the stabilization of their strategic relationship as a whole.[7] For this reason, India-China nuclear deterrence is relatively stable and poses no immediate nuclear risks.

But the same is not the case with the India–Pakistan nuclear dyad. Both countries have fought three major wars in 1947–8, 1965 and 1971 and a limited border war in 1999. They have also experienced several major crises that have created 'warlike situat-

[6] For more, see Michael J. Sullivan, 'Indian Attitudes on International Atomic Energy Controls', *Pacific Affairs*, Fall 1970, pp. 353–63.

[7] Rajesh Basrur, 'Nuclear India at Cross Roots', *Arms Control Today*, vol. 33, no. 7, September 2003, p. 8.

ions' in the subcontinent including a nine-month nuclear crisis in 2001–2. They still continue to adopt rigid postures on Kashmir and use dangerous strategies to check each other that could soon land them in another major war or create a warlike situation in the subcontinent. In this sense, the India–Pakistan nuclear relationship is inherently unstable and facilitates more immediate nuclear risks.

Nuclear Risks: The Indo–Pakistani Scenario

It is worthwhile to mention that there is a direct relationship between war or a near war situation and nuclear risks. Any war or warlike situation between India and Pakistan could raise three major nuclear risks: intentional use of nuclear weapons, accidental use of nuclear weapons, and unauthorized use of nuclear weapons. How could these occur? These are discussed as under.

Intentional Use of Nuclear Weapons

As discussed in the first chapter, India's and Pakistan's nuclear doctrines are diametrically opposed to each other. While India has declared a no-first-use nuclear policy, Pakistan, on the contrary, has favoured a 'nuclear first-use option'. Theoretically, a nuclear first-use policy has many risks and an NFU doctrine many virtues. For instance, a nuclear first-use policy could lead to increasing the size of the nuclear arsenals in a mutually debilitating arms race. It also requires hair-trigger alerts, launch-on warning and launch-through attack strategies and elaborate command and control, surveillance, early warning and intelligence systems with nuclear warheads loaded on launchers and ready to fire. These complex systems also increase the risk of accidents, unauthorized use, less-than-adequate control (as in the case of submarines) or use due to miscalculations.[8] An NFU policy not only solves many of the problems of nuclear first-use, it is also based on the belief that the fundamental purpose of nuclear weapons is to deter

[8] Jasjit Singh, 'Controlling the Nuclear Genie', *Indian Express*, 8 January 2003.

nuclear use and that nuclear weapons are not meant for war-fighting.

These two nuclear doctrines that are opposed to each other could have even been used for ensuring strategic stability in South Asia. For instance, Pakistan could have used its nuclear first-use policy, similar to Cold War Europe under North Atlantic Treaty Organisation (NATO), for maintaining the regional status quo and its own territorial integrity by countering a conventionally more powerful India. Similarly, India could have used its NFU doctrine to reassure Pakistan that it does not wish to threaten its conventionally weak neighbour. But as we will see below, this has not been the case. A significant element of the Pakistan Army leadership remains determined to overthrow the South Asian status quo by force. To achieve this, they are using their nuclear first-use policy to deter India from staging a conventional war in response to Pakistani military advances in Kashmir.[9] Similarly, India's NFU policy is being used to create a military-strategic space within which it could use its superior conventional force against Pakistan to fight a 'limited war under nuclear conditions'. The limited war view is premised on the notion that India has the ability to control every level of conflict, from conventional to battlefield, nuclear to strategic, and that any threat by Pakistan to use nuclear weapons first must take into account India's ability to raise the level of violence at every level, including the nuclear option.[10] These two dangerous policies are both escalatory and have the potential to result in a nuclear exchange. This probability is discussed as under.

Since the late 1980s when Pakistan acquired nuclear capability, it has pursued a proxy war in Kashmir without fear of Indian retaliation.[11] This proxy war, what has been described as the

[9] Farzana Shaikh, 'Pakistan's Nuclear Bomb: Beyond the Non-Proliferation Regime', *International Affairs*, vol. 78, no. 1, 2002, p. 37.

[10] Kanti Bajpai, 'No First Use in the India Pakistan Context', paper presented at the 279th Pugwash Meeting on South Asia, London, 15–17 November 2002.

[11] On using nuclear weapons as a shield for subconventional conflict, see Zia Mian, 'Renouncing the Nuclear Option', in *Pakistan and the Bomb*, ed. Samina Ahmed and David Cortright, Notre Dame: University of Notre Dame Press, 1998, pp. 62–4; Pervez Hoodbhoy, 'Pakistan's Nuclear Future', in *Pakistan and the Bomb*, ibid., pp. 70–2; and Shaikh, op. cit., n. 9 above, pp. 29–48.

'stability-instability' paradox,[12] is based on the logic that since Pakistan is protected by nuclear weapons, it is free to choose sub-conventional conflict with India. Fearing Pakistani first-use, India cannot cross the Line of Control (LOC) in Kashmir or the international boundary further as a way of punishing Pakistan for its interference in Kashmir.[13] As Jasjit Singh adds, 'It has been clear from the beginning that what Pakistan sought was not a nuclear war but a nuclear weapons umbrella under which to prosecute its proxy war in Jammu and Kashmir without the risk of Indian military retaliation.'[14] Perhaps this is a part of Pakistan's long-term strategy to 'bleed India with a thousand cuts' and force New Delhi to come to terms over Kashmir.

Over the years, the role of Pakistan in the military campaign in the state has undergone a radical transformation.[15] Initially, its role was limited to political, diplomatic and military support to the local Kashmiri militants. In the mid-1990s, militancy in the state was hijacked by foreign mercenaries with recruitment from as

[12] The stability-instability paradox states that rather than bringing stability to a pair of potential adversaries, nuclear weapons may create instability by encouraging one or both sides to engage in 'limited' military adventures against the other. These terms were coined by Glenn H. Snyder in 'The Balance of Power and the Balance of Terror' in The Balance of Power, ed. Paul Seabury, San Francisco: Chandler, 1965, pp. 184–201. For more, see Michael Krepon and Chris Gagne, eds., *The Stability-Instability Paradox: Nuclear Weapons and Brinkmanship in South Asia*, Report no. 35, Washington, DC: Stimson Center, June 2001; and Sumit Ganguly, 'Indo-Pakistani Nuclear Issues and the Stability-Instability Paradox', *Studies in Conflict and Terrorism*, vol. 18, 1995, pp. 325–34.

[13] Influential Pakistanis claim that Pakistan's nuclear capability deterred Indian conventional superiority thrice: in 1984, 1987, and 1990. See, for instance, Abdul Sattar, Agha Shahi and Zulfikar Ali Khan, 'Securing Nuclear Peace', *News International*, 5 October 1999.

[14] Jasjit Singh, 'The Wars that Never Were', *India Today*, 28 February 1984, p. 64.

[15] For an analysis of the origins of the 1989 Kashmir insurgency, see Sumit Ganguly, *The Crisis in Kashmir: Portents of War, Hopes of Peace*, Cambridge: Woodrow Wilson Center Press, 1999; and Upendra Choudhury, 'Internal in Security Under Seize: Need for Constitutional Correctives', in *Reviewing the Constitution*, ed. B.L. Fadia, New Delhi: Himanshu Publishers, 2001, pp. 138–78. For a discussion on Pakistan's changing tactics in Kashmir, see Askari Zaidi, 'Breaching the Line', *Times of India*, 15 June 1999.

many as fourteen Islamic nations allegedly controlled and guided by Pakistan.[16] After the open nuclear tests of May 1998, Pakistan's confidence that it could raise the conflict threshold with India increased with the direct involvement of its army to change the status quo in Kashmir that resulted in the Kargil War in 1999.[17] Islamabad's strategy was based on the premise that due to the new nuclear factor, international pressure would force the cessation of hostilities, leaving Pakistan in an advantageous position on the ground. This strategy not only failed miserably, but the Kargil debacle caused political turmoil in Pakistan. Army Chief General Pervez Musharraf led the military coup in October 1999. The military leadership convinced itself that it would have won the Kargil War were it not for the pusillanimity of the Nawaz Sharif Government. This type of rationalization led to a substantial rise in violence and killings in Jammu & Kashmir by the Pakistan-based terrorist organizations. This included *fidayeen* (suicide) attack on Indian military and paramilitary forces, installations and administrative headquarters in Kashmir.

In December 1999, terrorists based in Pakistan hijacked an Indian Airlines aircraft IC-814 to Kandahar and forced the release of three associates imprisoned for terrorist activity in Kashmir.[18] Moreover, groups directly linked to Pakistan have perpetrated even more intolerable attacks against India. Two such incidents are noteworthy. On 1 October 2001, the Pakistan-based terrorists outfits Laskar-e-Toiba and Jaish-e-Muhammed (which were soon designated as terrorist organizations by the US) organized a brazen assault on the Kashmir state legislature. Similarly, on 13 December 2001, an even bolder attack on the Indian Parliament took place.

[16] Rajesh Ramchandran's interview with M.K. Narayan, *Hindustan Times*, 2 January 2000.

[17] For a discussion on the causes and consequences of the Kargil War, see CCC Conference Report, *Asymmetric Conflict in South Asia: The Causes and Consequences of the 1999 Limited War in Kargil*, 29 May–1 June 2002, Monterey, California.

[18] The three hard-core terrorists released in exchange for the IC-814 hostages included Maulana Masood Azhar (who later established the JeM), Ahmed Umar Saeed Sheikh, and Mushtaq Ahmed Zargar.

These terrorist attacks, especially the Parliament assault, triggered the deployment of Indian forces on the border with Pakistan.[19]

Although violence has been in steady decline since 2001—because of India's threat to go to war, US pressure on Islamabad and the recent dialogue between India and Pakistan—it has not completely stopped. Infiltration, as then Indian Army Chief Nirmal Vij stated, resumed.[20] US Deputy Secretary of State, Richard Armitage admitted in New Delhi that Pakistan had yet to dismantle the infrastructure of jihadi terror there.[21] A recent Indian Home Ministry document has revealed that the Inter-Services Intelligence (ISI) has reopened militant training camps in large numbers in Pak-Occupied Kashmir (POK), including the northern areas.[22]

Pakistan's continuous cross-border terrorist activity has brought a radical reorientation of security strategy in India. This new strategy, called the doctrine of 'limited war' under nuclear conditions,[23] germinated after the Kargil conflict of 1999 and the rising tide of terrorist violence in Kashmir and elsewhere in the post-Kargil period.

It is worth mentioning that ever since South Asia was nuclearized, Indian policy makers believed that nuclear weapons demanded great caution, and the use of force in the India–Pakistan relationship was ruled out. However, the shock of the Kargil conflict and the growing sense of being tied down by the constraints of being a Nuclear Weapon State (NWS) despite overwhelming conventional military superiority, led to a rethinking

[19] For more, see V.K. Sood and Pravin Sawhney, *Operation Parakram: The Unfinished War*, New Delhi: Sage, 2003.

[20] Praveen Swami, 'Peace on the Guillotine Again', *Hindu*, 19 July 2004.

[21] Ibid.

[22] 'ISI Still Trains Ultras in POK: MHA', *Indian Express*, 21 June 2004; also see 'Punjab, Sindh Mein 'Jehadi' Recruitment Centres' ('Jehadi' Recruitment Centres in Punjab, Sindh), *Hindu*, 12 July 2004.

[23] For an understanding of the history of limited war, see Suba Chandran, 'An Enquiry Into Limited War' at: http://www.ipcs.org/ipcs/issue/index2.isp?action=Show View&kvalue=799&issue=1011&status=article&mode=b; for an account of India's Limited War Doctrine, see Jasjit Singh, 'Dynamics of Limited War', *Strategic Analysis*, vol. XXIV, no. 7, October 2000, pp. 1205–20; and V.R. Raghavan, 'Nuclear Weapons and New Wars', *Hindu*, 6 October 1998.

of Indian strategy, a search for 'strategic space' between inaction and nuclear war.[24] Moreover, political leaders, government officials, military leaders and a groundswell of public opinion including the media and think tanks, all supported a change in government policy towards Pakistan and advocated ending the Pakistani threat once and for all, by war if necessary.

What exactly is meant by 'limited war' is not officially articulated, but we can enumerate some of its basic assumptions from the speeches of political and military leaders and writings of independent strategic experts. These are as follows:

- Nuclear weapons 'can deter only the use of nuclear weapons but not all or any war'.[25]
- Strategic space exists between the low-intensity war waged by Pakistan and nuclear escalation. It is in the strategic space below nuclear exchange where conventional military power is to be applied. The 1999 Kargil war and the Sino–Soviet war of 1969 are cited as examples.
- While India's nuclear second-strike will counter Pakistani nuclear first-use (it is believed that Pakistan will be circumspect in resorting to nuclear weapons because of the immense potential damage to itself that may result), India's superior conventional forces will be used to carry out a limited conventional operation.
- This operation will be a sharp, swift, small and quick one without threatening Pakistani interests so greatly as to invite a nuclear strike.[26]
- If that turns out to be a miscalculation and Pakistan initiates the use of nuclear weapons, then India would retaliate and 'Pakistan could cease to exist'.[27]

[24] Rajesh Basrur, 'Kargil, Terrorism and India's Strategic Shift', *India Review*, vol. 1, no. 4, October 2002, pp. 39–56.

[25] 'Fernandes Unveils "Limited War" Doctrine', *Hindu*, 25 January 2000.

[26] Jasjit Singh, 'Doctrine and Strategy Under the Nuclear Umbrella', *Indian Express*, 5 June 2004.

[27] Indian official quoted in 'Crisis in South Asia', *New Yorker*, 8 January 2002, p. 40.

Thus, India's limited war doctrine seeks to undermine Pakistan's use of the stability–instability paradox—the use of nuclear deterrence to export terrorism—and convince Islamabad that nuclear deterrence would not deter New Delhi from military action, and that Pakistan's support to terrorism in India would henceforth carry costs.

The 11 September 2001 terrorist attack on the American World Trade Center in New York that led to a global revulsion against terrorism and the further intensification of terrorist activity in Jammu & Kashmir (especially the October attack on the state legislature) further crystallized the new Indian strategy. But the threshold of India's tolerance was breached when Pakistan-based terrorists attacked the national Parliament in December 2001. This was followed by the massing of troops by India, and subsequently by Pakistan along their border, raising the fear of another war in South Asia.[28] This crisis resulted in 'Operation Parakram' only to be averted by the active role of the USA.

Pakistan's continuous terrorist activity against India has escalation risks that could result in a nuclear exchange between New Delhi and Islamabad. Although the present Pakistani strategy is based on the assumption that war through terrorism does not go beyond a level where India might be tempted or forced to escalate (it did after the Parliament attack), yet several factors could lead to nuclear escalation. First, the presence of armed militant groups in Pakistan and their influence in the military is a factor that can contribute to escalation.[29] No doubt, the militants are a small group yet as they

[28] For more, see Achin Vanaik, 'Deterrence or a Deadly Game? Nuclear Propaganda and Reality in South Asia', *Disarmament Diplomacy*, no. 61, September 2002, at: http://www.acronym.org.uk/dd/dd66/66op3.htm; T. S. Gopi Rethinaraj, 'Threats and Perceptions of Nuclear War in South Asia', *Swords and Ploughshares*, vol. XIV, no. 1, Summer 2002, pp. 22–5; and V. R. Raghavan, 'Manipulating Nuclear Deterrent', *Hindu*, 3 July 2002.

[29] For more on this aspect, see Neil Joeck, *Maintaining Nuclear Stability in South Asia*, Adelphi Paper no. 312, London: IISS, 1997, pp. 16–20; Vanaik, ibid.; Michael Krepon, 'The Jihadis Make it Worse', *Hindu*, 1 January 2002; and Siddharth Varadarajan, 'On the Precipice: Beware, the Terrorist's Trap', *Times of India*, 8 May 2002. Also see Massoud Ansari, 'The Jehad Factories', *Frontline*, vol. 18, no. 16, 17 August 2001, pp. 65–70; Satish Kumar, 'Militant Islam: The Nemesis of Pakistan, *Strategic Digest*, vol. XXX, no. 8, August 2000, pp. 1075–87; Sumita Kumar, 'Pakistan's

are the country's primary means of exerting pressure in Kashmir, they enjoy greater support in the country's armed forces. It should not be forgotten that these are the same jihadis who, during the Kargil war, said 'Have we produced them (nuclear weapons) as toys for exhibitions?'[30] Second, public pronouncements from both sides about the conflict (either on Kargil or about the 2002 crisis) are not encouraging. They consist largely of each side's claims that it got the better of the other because it possessed nuclear deterrence.[31] No one can be sure which view is true, but misplaced confidence on both sides continues to make the situation extremely volatile. Third, Pakistan's terrorism policy has encouraged India to acquire new military systems and devise new military doctrines. For instance, Pakistan's thoughtless policy has led some elements in India to argue that New Delhi should acquire Anti-Ballistic Missile (ABM) systems to degrade a Pakistani nuclear strike against its forces and thereby induce Pakistan to desist from its continued support to insurgents in Kashmir and elsewhere.[32] Similarly, according to press reports, the Indian Army, on the basis of the lessons of Kargil (where the troops did not cross the LOC) and Operation Parakram (where no military action was taken) has recommended to the government to exploit Pakistan's perception that India does not have the national will to strike to achieve surprise and deception.[33] This perception, that could have far-

---

Jihadi Apparatus: Goals and Methods', *Strategic Analysis*, vol. XXIV, no. 2, March 2001, pp. 2179–98; Ajay Darshan Behera, 'The Supporting Structures for Pakistan's Proxy War in J&K', *Strategic Analysis*, vol. XXV, no. 3, June 2001, pp. 393–410; and Jessica Stern, 'Pakistan's Jihad Culture', *Foreign Affairs*, vol. 79, no. 6, November–December 2000, pp. 115–26.

[30] Quoted in Samuel Baid, 'Pakistan: Nuclear Power and Jihadi Commitments', *Daily Excelsior* (Jammu), 1 October 2002.

[31] 'We Defeated "Enemy" Without a War: Musharraf', *Hindu*, 14 December 2002. Also see Raja Menon, 'Dangerous Deductions', *Indian Express*, 26 December 2002.

[32] See, for instance, C. Raja Mohan, 'Next Steps in Missile Defence', *Indian Express*, 10 February 2004.

[33] 'Pak Studying Cold Start Doctrine of Indian Army', *Indian Express*, 10 June 2004, p. 7.

reaching implications on shaping future Indian military strategy, according to the Army, should be reinforced as a strategy to achieve the elements of surprise in a war with Pakistan. In other words, the Pakistani perception of India's inability to strike it back can be reinforced as a strategy by launching a short, quick and surprise attack against that country without giving Pakistan an opportunity to resort to nuclear first use. The Army also wants the government to clearly enunciate its specific response to tactical nuclear weapons to deter the adversary. It has also recommended that the government review its nuclear, biological and chemical (NBC) policies in the light of 'specific threats made by Pakistan-based terrorists on using Weapons of Mass Destruction (WMD) against India'.

The belief in India that a limited war against Pakistan can be fought or won despite the presence of nuclear weapons is equally dangerous.[34] The reasons are not difficult to find. The first relates to the confidence among many Indians that a limited war will remain limited or at best halted at conventional levels. Studies during the Cold War and analysis of results from the many war games conducted by other nuclear states have indicated that any restraint on war without a mutual understanding to do so would be a near impossibility.[35] Even in the nine-month military standoff of 2001–2, there were reports that both India and Pakistan had deployed nuclear weapons. Second, war by its nature favours escalation. This is why during the 2002 crisis, Indian generals could not promise that a limited war against Pakistan would not go 'nuclear', and the political leadership concluded that the risks of such a war were too great. To quote Atal Behari Vajpayee, 'The problem with starting a war is that you never know how it will end and you never know where it will end.'[36] Third, India's limited

[34] For an excellent discussion on many problems of limited war, see V.R. Raghavan, 'Limited War and Nuclear Escalation in South Asia', *Non-Proliferation Review*, vol. VIII, no. 3, Fall–Winter 2001, pp. 82–98; and Suba Chandran, 'Limited War: Unlimited Questions' at: http://www.ipcs.org/ipcs/issue/index2.isp?action=ShowView&kvalue=80&issue=1011&status=article&mod=6

[35] Raghavan, ibid., p. 96.

[36] Atal Behari Vajpayee, quoted by British Foreign Secretary Jack Straw in his interview with Sekhar Gupta, *Indian Express*, 22 February 2005, p. 9.

political and military objectives could be viewed as unlimited and unacceptable by Pakistan. India–Pakistan history is, in fact, replete with asymmetrical perceptions, strategic miscalculations and divergent definitions of the 'unacceptable'.[37] Last, it is very hard to imagine that serious full-scale conventional warfare would go on for long without one side or the other succumbing to the pressure and temptations of the situation.

India's limited war doctrine is based on a desire to avoid threatening Pakistan's 'core interests', thereby inviting a nuclear response. There are a number of problems with this. First, what according to Pakistan are its core interests cannot be known with certainty. Second, many in India believe that Pakistan has an interest in taking the conflict towards a nuclear flashpoint as early as possible, perhaps to force intervention by the international community. Third, Pakistan's Army has an institutional interest in maintaining its pre-eminence in that country's power structure. This cannot be maintained if it is militarily defeated at the hands of India in a limited conventional war. To avoid conflict, it may respond in a way that it subsequently finds it has to defend by nuclear means. Given the empirical evidence of the Pakistan Army's past behaviour (it has acted irrationally in the past, leading the country into disastrous experiences in 1965 and 1971), such a possibility cannot be ruled out.[38] Last, the Indian strategy of not threatening Pakistan's core interests and quickly achieving the war objectives could inadvertently encourage a more rapid and possibly less considered nuclear response from Pakistan.[39]

Moreover, it is naive to expect that nuclear decisions in a war situation would be based on a rational assessment, because in an armed conflict between two NWS, 'decision makers would be functioning under a high level of stress with imperfect information,

[37] Praful Bidwai, 'From Pokhran to Kargil: The Nuclear Danger is No Fantasy', *Times of India*, 2 June 1999.

[38] For more on this, see Timothy D. Hoyt, 'Pakistan's Nuclear Doctrine and Dangers of Strategic Myopia', *Asian Survey*, vol. XLI, no. 6, November–December 2001, pp. 956–77; and C. Uday Bhaskar, 'Lifting the Smoke Screen: Terror Tales From Pakistan Army', *Times of India*, 3 January 2003.

[39] Raghavan, op. cit., n. 34 above, p. 90.

exaggerated threat perceptions and worst-case assumptions'.[40] Public outcry, a political need to demonstrate strength, military pressure, and the pressure of the scientific lobby could all affect decision making with the potential to reach the nuclear threshold. What is more deplorable is that neither Pakistan nor India seems to have learnt any lesson from their past crises. Both sides still believe that they can sooner or later achieve their objectives by persisting in their present approaches.[41] India hopes to contain and ultimately defeat outside militancy by using its superior military might without crossing into Pakistan. Pakistan, on its part, feels it can force India into negotiations aimed at giving up Kashmir by indulging in its low-cost instigation of violence.

Thus, we have a vicious circle here. The more India thinks that Pakistan is using its first-strike threat to promote cross-border terrorism, the more it will move in the direction of limited war under nuclear conditions to indicate that Pakistan is not immune from retaliation. The more India is seen to move in this direction, the more Pakistan will emphasize its nuclear first-use. The more it does so, the more it will increase the importance of Indian second-strike nuclear threats, thereby resulting in a nuclear exchange in the region.

Accidental Nuclear Use

Nuclear weapons placed on alert during a crisis are prone to accident and accidental use. This could happen in two ways. The first is the possibility of nuclear weapons use in the event of a miscalculation. An example could be undertaking conventional military movements that are not intended to promote a nuclear response but do. This possibility has been discussed towards the end of this chapter (pp. 55–6).

The second is the possibility of a nuclear launch on the basis of misinterpretation. A non-threatening event might be misinter-

[40] Feroz Hasan Khan, 'Challenges to Nuclear Stability in South Asia', *Non-Proliferation Review*, vol. X, no. 1, Spring 2003, p. 67.

[41] K. Shankar Bajpai, 'Untangling India and Pakistan', *Foreign Affairs*, vol. 82, no. 3, May–June 2003, p. 113.

preted as an attack and lead to a nuclear response.[42] This could occur in normal times too, but its probability is much greater in the midst of a serious crisis due to lack of early warning information or the presence of faulty early warning data. Two examples can drive home the point.

First, a nuclear accident that takes place in times of crisis may be misinterpreted as an attack, initiating a nuclear war. A nuclear accident could occur because the design of the nuclear weapon itself is faulty, or because the systems and procedures used to launch or drop the weapons lack safeguards such as shortcomings in their storage, handling, transportation, maintenance, and testing, among other thing..[43]

It is not clear whether India's and Pakistan's nuclear programmes, still in the early stages of development, without too many tests under their belt, carry such design-level safety (safety measures built into the design of weapons).[44] Moreover, mechanical and electrical malfunctions that could result in a nuclear accident are well within the realm of possibility. Any survey of the past record of the performance of India and Pakistan shows how routine their technology failures are.[45]

A second example of how mistaken human interpretation of incomplete data could lead to a serious situation relates to the Pakistani nuclear tests of May 1998. Prior to Prime Minister Nawaz

[42] For more, see Shirin Tahir-Kheli and Kent L. Biringer, 'Reducing Risk in South Asia: Managing India-Pakistan Tensions', CMC Occasional Paper, at: http://www.cmc.sandia.gov/Links/about/papers/SAND98-0505/20/index.html

[43] A recent example of a serious accident involving a missile occurred on 23 February 2004 at the Sriharikota High Altitude Range. Engineers were testing a motor for the Agni missile when it caught fire and exploded, killing at least six persons. If such an accident were to occur in a liquid fuelled Prithvi missile loaded with a nuclear warhead, the consequences could be catastrophic. See M.V. Ramana and R. Rajaraman, 'Reducing Nuclear Risk', *Hindu*, 4 June 2004.

[44] R. Rajaraman, M.V. Ramana and Zia Mian, 'Possession and Deployment of Nuclear Weapons in South Asia: An Assessment of Some Risks', *Economic and Political Weekly*, 22 June 2002, p. 2463, at: http://www.geocities.com/m_v_ramana/nucleararticles/epw_deploymentrisks.htm

[45] For more, see Zia Mian, M.V. Ramana and R. Rajaraman, 'Risks and Consequences of Nuclear Weapon Accidents in South Asia', *Current Science*, vol. 80, no. 10, 2001, pp. 1275–84.

Sharif's decision to go ahead with the nuclear tests, the ISI officers told him that the Indian and Israeli Air Forces were about to launch a pre-emptive strike on the test site. The small Pakistani missile arsenal was said to have been placed on a high state of alert because of this report.[46] This incident and the earlier example serve as a warning that the danger of accidental war—caused by false warning—is likely to be a serious nuclear risk in South Asia despite the recent efforts of the two countries, especially India, to overcome this problem by going for sophisticated early warnings systems.[47]

The false warning problem is further complicated by the factor of geography. The missile travel time between India and Pakistan is only about five minutes. This is too short a time to permit any sensible decision-making on nuclear matters.

Risk of Unauthorized Nuclear Use

Following a crisis, if nuclear weapons are deployed and on full alert, there are risks that unauthorized persons could use them. There are two scenarios for this. The first is use by a rogue commander (a commander who takes control of the nuclear forces he commands), and the second is use by terrorists.

NUCLEAR USE BY A ROGUE COMMANDER

Both India and Pakistan have established command and control systems that are supposed to avert the unauthorized use of nuclear

[46] Scott D. Sagan, 'Nuclear Safety and Security in South Asia', in *Proliferation Challenges and Non-Proliferation Opportunity for New Administration*, ed. Michael Barletta, CNS Occasional Paper no. 4, Monterey Institute of International Studies (MIIS), 2000, p. 38.

[47] According to press reports, for the last few years India has been acquiring the key components of an early warning network, including the Green Pine radar from Israel. However, it may be noted that early warning systems are often prone to false alarms and create the risk of inadvertent launch through failure of technology. Moreover, these systems simply cannot offer more than a few minutes of warning, which is grossly insufficient for decision making in any meaningful sense of the term. See Zia Mian, R. Rajaraman and M.V. Ramana, 'When Early Warning is No Warning', *Hindu*, 2 July 2004; also see 'Shalom India', *Times of India*, 7 September 2003.

weapons. Even the most advanced command and control systems are, however, not foolproof. Besides, it can be assumed that during a hot crisis that escalates to a point where central political decision makers decide to deploy nuclear weapons, it would be natural for them to disperse not just deployed nuclear weapons and their delivery systems as widely as possible, but also delegate their command and control to the field commanders, allowing them to make the vital decision about using nuclear weapons. This is essential in order to avoid vulnerability to a nuclear first-strike. Pakistan has one more reason to do so due to lack of its strategic depth.

Once nuclear weapons are deployed and dispersed, the political and military demands on command and control systems would become acute. Similarly, central communications to dispersed nuclear units would become both technically demanding and politically essential. Although the chain of command is clearly spelled out under all military contingencies, in the event of a command, control and communication breakdown following the large-scale effects of a nuclear war, the theatre commander, seeing the opponent's forces marching in, would likely take matters into his own hands.[48] Moreover, a military commander who believes in heavenly benefits is quite capable of launching a nuclear missile even if he knows that a devastating response is certain.

Nuclear Use by Terrorists

Unauthorized use of nuclear weapons by terrorists remains a significant risk during a war or a crisis. In fact, one may contribute to the other. However, it should be made clear that terrorists are unlikely to be able to manufacture an operational nuclear weapon of their own given the difficulties involved in obtaining the required facilities and technical know-how. Nevertheless, they

[48] The many hazards of command and control for South Asia are discussed in Zia Mian, 'A Nuclear Tiger by the Tail: Problems of Command and Control in South Asia' in *Prisons of the Nuclear Dream*, ed. M.V. Ramana and C. Rammanohar Reddy, New Delhi: Orient Longman, 2003. Also see Clayton Bowen and Danial Wolven, 'Command and Control Challenges in South Asia', *Non-Proliferation Review*, vol.VI, no. 3, Spring-Summer 1999, pp. 25–35.

have the ability to carry out less devastating forms of attack. As President George Bush of the United States has rightly remarked, the greatest danger we face is that 'the world's most dangerous people' will get their hands on the 'world's most dangerous weapons'.[49]

Both India and Pakistan are believed to keep their nuclear weapons in an unassembled form under normal circumstances. In such a situation, the probability of terrorist groups acquiring fully operational nuclear weapons does not arise. This situation may, however, change during a war or tense military stand-off when India and Pakistan feel it imperative to deploy and disperse their nuclear weapons. Should that happen, the process of transportation and deployment of warheads would create fresh targets for terrorists.[50] Notwithstanding the extensive precautions that New Delhi and Islamabad might take for their nuclear assets, the probability of security breaches remains high. After all, we have not forgotten that terrorists have penetrated and launched attacks in high-security zones such as Army camps, ammunition dumps, the national Parliament, among others.

Terrorist ability to carry out devastating attacks could also spark a nuclear war or a hot crisis. For instance, a terrorist might sabotage a nuclear facility to release lethal radiation. Similarly, he could utilize a 'dirty bomb' to disperse radiation. In either case, the government involved would have to quickly determine whether the radiation release was accidental or deliberate. If these took place at a moment of very high tension, they could precipitate a chain of events leading to still more serious steps.

Paul Leventhal and Brahma Chellaney have cited four reasons for nuclear terrorism in South Asia in 1988: the rapidly expanding nuclear programmes of India and Pakistan; their growing stockpiles of nuclear materials; the enduring problem of terrorism faced by both countries; and the increasing tactical sophistication

[49] Bush, quoted in Fareed Zakaria, 'Deaf to a Ticking Bomb', *Indian Express*, 16 June 2004.

[50] Rajesh Basrur and Hasan Askari Rizvi, *Nuclear Terrorism and South Asia*, CMC Occasional Paper, February 2003, Albuquerque, USA: CMC, Sandia National Laboratories, p. 62.

of terrorists.[51] These are relevant even today. Besides, there are some other reasons why terrorists could indulge in such horrific attacks. First, despite the progress made in capturing terrorists and disrupting their networks, the terrorist threat in South Asia is likely to remain for some time. Second, Indo–Pakistani nuclear and missile installations are protected against aerial raids by enemy countries. They have deployed the best of their anti-aircraft missiles, interceptor planes and low-detecting radar around their nuclear facilities. Ground protection in most, if not all, nuclear facilities is 'left to barbed wires and primitively armed civilian personnel'.[52] This could result in nuclear theft and smuggling and sabotage by terrorists. Third, numerous cases of theft clearly increase such a risk. For instance, a significant theft of radiological material occurred in August 2003 at a research lab in the Indian state of Jharkhand.[53] A similar case was reported from the Indira Gandhi Centre for Atomic Research in Chennai in July 1998.[54] Last, today's terrorists are motivated by religious rather than political goals. They believe that they are fighting for a 'sacred cause'. Were such individuals to ever acquire nuclear, biological and chemical WMDs, they would accept the possibility of the annihilation of their lives, the lives of their fellow men and even their own nation if they could believe that the 'Empire of God' could be expanded.[55]

There are two additional risks in the case of Pakistan. First, Pakistan might experience serious political instability in future. Political instability affects nuclear stability in two ways. Once there is internal turmoil, there will be a breakdown of security around

[51] Paul Leventhal and Brahma Chellaney, 'Nuclear Terrorism: Threat Perception and Response in South Asia' at: http://www.nci.org/nci-use.htm

[52] R. Prasannan, 'Musharraf's Nightmares', *Week*, vol. 19, no. 49, 11 November 2001, pp. 42–6. For more on this aspect, also see Sasmita Tripathy, 'Nuclear Terrorism in South Asia: Threat and Response', paper presented at the 52nd All India Political Science Association, Ch. Charan Singh University, Meerut, 10–12 October 2003.

[53] Michael Krepon, 'Moving from Crisis to Nuclear Safety', *Hindu*, 5 February 2004.

[54] 'Uranium Racket Unearthed', *Indian Express*, 23 July 2002; also see 'Bid to Sell Nuclear Secrets Began in 1990s', *Hindu*, 16 May 2004.

[55] K.P.S. Gill, 'Technology, Terror and a Thoughtless State', *Faultlines*, vol. 3, at: http://www.satp.org/satporgtp/publication/faultlines/volume3/index.html

nuclear forces, weapons areas, storage locations or development facilities that will allow terrorists to gain control of nuclear materials or weapons. These can be called command and control problems. Second, there is the question of perception. Political instability in one state may raise the prospect in the minds of its adversary that a moment of great opportunity or danger is approaching.

Pakistan has been plagued by political instability for more than a decade and a half. Although stability is provided by the steel frame of its army that is still a disciplined force and functions with a clear chain of command, yet there are signs that all is not well in it. There is increasing discontent within the Pakistani armed forces with a significant section now opposing their president's policy of appeasing the 'West'.[56] This section dominates largely the second tier of the Army and has been a consistent source of pressure against adopting pro-Western policies, specially the military operations under US pressure against alleged terrorists and their Pakistani supporters in the tribal areas of South Waziristan along the Pakistan and Afghanistan borders. Anti-Musharraf pamphlets are being circulated within the Armed Forces establishment. In fact, there have been several suicide attacks on Musharraf himself by Army and Air Force personnel.[57] There is evidence of arbitrary arrests of officers whose loyalty and discipline have been suspected.

Moreover, it is alleged that the Pakistan Army has been penetrated by jihadi elements. The number of bearded officers and men is growing. They have close links with the hardline Islamic parties that won unprecedented victories in the October 2002 elections. Never in the history of Pakistan had the fundamentalists gained more than 2–3 per cent seats in the National Assembly, but in 2002, they gained 20 per cent. Besides, they have become the ruling combine in the North-West Frontier Province (NWFP) and the leading political force in Baluchistan.[58] This deadly combi-

[56] G. Parthasarathy, 'Enemy in the Ranks', *Indian Express*, 21 June 2004.

[57] 'Karachi's Killing Fields', *Indian Express*, 12 June 2004. Also see Benazir Bhutto, 'The CEOs of Terror', *Indian Express*, 5 May 2004.

[58] For more, see Suba Chandran, 'Rise of Religious Parties in Pak', *Hindu*, 29 November 2002.

nation of political and military forces could pose a growing threat to the Musharraf regime. Should the Musharraf Government be toppled, Pakistan's nuclear weapons could come under the control of the new regime of possibly more radical Islamic elements.

The Central Intelligence Agency (CIA) report entitled 'Global Trends 2015' ominously noted in 2001 that 'Pakistan will not recover easily from decades of political and economic mismanagement, divisive politics and ethnic feuds. In a climate of continuing domestic turmoil, the central government's control will probably be reduced to the Punjab heartland and the economic hub of Karachi.'[59] Similarly, Professor in Stephen Cohen, an eminent South Asian analyst, remarks:

> Its (Pakistan's) non-Punjabi provinces are deeply resentful, its economy is teetering on the edge of collapse, it has undergone a traumatic reversal of policy in Afghanistan and its political parties seemed to be struck in their personality rut. There is no credible civilian leadership emerging among the younger generation of politicians and the two civilian leaders of the 1990s, Benazir Bhutto and Nawaz Sharif are distrusted by the military.[60]

A second risk concerns the reliability and trustworthiness of its scientists, technicians and military people, those who have the responsibility of handling the nuclear weapons and fissile materials. In recent months, Pakistan has faced the accusation accused that its scientists are involved in the large-scale transfer of sensitive nuclear technologies and materials to Iran, North Korea and Libya.[61] The most controversial scientist is A.Q. Khan—the hero of Pakistan's nuclear bomb. Khan recently confessed that he has

[59] CIA Report, 'Global Trends 2015', 2001, at: http://www.odci.gov/cia/reports/globaltrends2015/index.html

[60] Stephen Philip Cohen, 'Nuclear Weapons and Nuclear War in South Asia: An Unknowable Future', paper presented to the UN University Conference on South Asia, Tokyo, May 2002, at: http://www.brook.edu/dybdocroot/views /speeches/cohens20020501.pdf

[61] For more, see Praful Bidwai, 'Closing the Global Nuclear Bazaar, *Frontline*, vol. 21, no. 4, 27 February 2004, pp. 127–9; V. S. Arunachalam, 'Proliferation and After', *Hindu*, 13 February 2004; and Gaurav Kampani, 'Second Tier Proliferation: The Case of Pakistan and North Korea', *Non-Proliferation Review*, vol. 9, no. 3, Fall–Winter 2002, pp. 107–16.

for quite sometime been operating an elaborate international network for the transfer of nuclear weapon designs, material and technologies from Pakistan. This network is now considered as one of the most well-organized, complex and relatively successful networks in the world to smuggle nuclear weapons technology to other countries. Two theses are offered to explain the A.Q. Khan revelations. One (favoured by many in the US and India), argues that it is unbelievable that proliferation on such a large scale could occur without the knowledge of the Pakistan Army, which presently governs that country. The other, heard in Pakistan, contends that Khan was a 'rogue actor' who abused the autonomy he gained from his earlier patriotic actions to pursue personal goals.[62] The evidence, however, is clearly against the second. It is common knowledge that the Army has been the underwriter and protector of the Pakistani nuclear programme since its very inception. Therefore, it is naïve to believe that it is not directly responsible for what has happened. Moreover, the immediate public pardon of Khan without any trial further confirms this. Mohmed El-Baradei, the IAEA chief, correctly states that the information on Khan was just the 'tip of the iceberg', and that the Pakistani nuclear scientist was not alone in spreading nuclear technology.[63]

Equally of concern is the discovery of the linkage between Pakistani nuclear scientists and the Al-Qaida elements. This does not create much confidence in the reliability of Pakistan's Personnel Reliability Programme (PRP)[64]—that ensures the involvement of responsible people for nuclear weapons management. In October 2002, the Pakistan government arrested two of its nuclear scientists and questioned them regarding contacts they had with Laden's network. In view of all this, it appears that there is a real risk of

[62] Christopher Clary, 'Dr Khan's Nuclear WalMart', *Disarmament Diplomacy*, no. 76, March–April 2004.

[63] Quoted in B. Muralidhar Reddy, 'Nuclear Home Truths', *Frontline*, vol. 21, no. 4, 27 February 2004, pp. 45–7.

[64] 'Pak Nuclear Scientists in Touch With Al-Qaeda', *Tribune*, 23 October 2002; also see 'AQ Claims to Possess Smart Briefcase Nuclear Bombs', *Hindu*, 22 March 2004.

sensitive nuclear material or even weapons components falling into terrorist hands by the Pakistani state or it's own renegade nuclear scientists.[65]

Could there be more nuclear risks once India and Pakistan expand their nuclear weapon programmes? Although there are reports that both New Delhi and Islamabad have been making the fissile material (the nuclear explosives) for their weapons as fast as they can for decades,[66] yet it should be mentioned that barring a serious negative turn in its relationship with Pakistan and China or the emergence of an unanticipated threat, the pace of India's nuclear evolution is likely to be glacial. After all, India has repeatedly stated that it will not match bomb for bomb or missile for missile. This is equally true for Pakistan, as its nuclear policy is generally reactive to India's. If, however, there is a significant deterioration in India's security environment, New Delhi's thinking and practice may change. This, in turn, may encourage Pakistan to follow suit. If both countries, as a result, go for a large nuclear arsenal, there would be more nuclear accidents, command and control problems, and more targets for the terrorists.

Pakistan faces another typical problem. Unlike India, it does not have the luxury of strategic depth. Its nuclear assets are located close to the border, vulnerable to attack even by conventional forces. They are also at risk of coming into direct contact with conventional combat operations during wartime,[67] which could,

[65] For more, see Narayanan Komerath, 'Has Pakistan Lost Its Nuclear Weapons?', *Bharat Rakshak Monitor*, vol. 5, no. 1, July–August 2002, at: http://www.bharat-rakshak.com/MONOTOR/ISSUES5-1/narayanan.html; News Review, 'Concern Over Pakistan's Nuclear Weapons', *Disarmament Diplomacy*, no. 61, October–November 2001; Amit Barua, 'A. Khan for Osama Deal', *Hindu*, 8 March 2004; and K. Santhanam and Rajesh Rajagopalan, 'Security of Pakistan's Nuclear Arsenal', *Hindu*, 12 November 2001.

[66] Zia Mian, A.H. Nayyar and M.V. Ramana, 'Making Weapons Talking Peace: Resolving Dilemma of Nuclear Negotiations', *Economic and Political Weekly*, 17 July 2004, pp. 3221–4.

[67] For more on this aspect, see Stephen Smith, 'Assessing the Risk of Inadvertent Nuclear War between India and Pakistan', Masters dissertation, Naval Post-Graduate School, Monterey, California, December 2002, at: http://www.ccc.nps.navy.mil/research/these/smith02.asp

in turn, compel a hasty decision to 'use them' out of fear that they were about to be captured or destroyed. Similarly, Pakistan firmly believes that India, despite its repeated pronouncements of a second-strike policy, would contemplate attacking first in a crisis, perhaps to destroy Pakistan's nuclear weapons capability. Therefore, Pakistan is likely to disperse and delegate as it operationalizes its nuclear arsenal. This would create more dangerous situations, including the possibility of a 'rogue launch'.

Nuclear Risks: The India–China Scenario

As mentioned earlier, the India–China nuclear dyad is relatively more stable than the India–Pakistan nuclear relationship. But this does not mean that there are or would be no nuclear risks. This can be analysed by examining India's and China's threat perceptions towards each other, and explaining the probability of war between these two countries on the basis of this divergent threat perceptions.

From the Chinese perspective, there are a number of issues that hamper a truly stable Sino–Indian relationship. First, India has maintained an aggressive drive toward its northern boundary and has occupied some 90,000 sq. km. of Chinese territory since its independence from Britain in 1947.[68] In 1962, India continued to pursue what the Chinese call 'a policy of expansionism', which triggered an invasion by China. The second is the controversy surrounding Tibet.[69] The official Chinese news agency Xinhua reported that the Indian government tried in vain to obstruct China's liberation of Tibet but continues to provide the Dalai Lama a site to launch campaigns in support of Tibetan separatism.[70] Some Chinese even argue that India's security interests demand Tibet to be separated from China to form a buffer zone, thus

[68] Ming Zhang, *China's Changing Nuclear Posture: Reactions to the South Asian Nuclear Tests*, Washington, DC: Carnegie Endowment for International Peace Paper, 1999, p. 15, at: http://www.ceip.org/pubs/china-zhang/CH2.PDF

[69] Dawa Norbu, 'Tibet in Sino-Indian Relations: The Centrality of Marginality', *Asian Survey*, vol. 37, no. 11, November 1997, pp. 1078–95.

[70] Cited in Zhang, op. cit., n. 68 above, pp. 14–15.

removing a direct threat from China and allowing India greater freedom in the subcontinent.[71] Another Chinese concern is India's reluctance to follow China in signing the CTBT and to keep its nuclear option open. The use of a China threat by India to justify its 1998 nuclear tests and its continuing refusal to sign the CTBT, create, in Chinese eyes, new threats to China's southern border security.[72] Chinese analysts, specially those affiliated with the military, are also concerned with India's continued missile development and its resolve to achieve a credible minimum deterrent based on a strategic triad.[73] They add that the more India continues to move towards acquiring the capability to strike deep into China's heartland, the more Beijing is likely to reassess its nuclear posture and missile deployment vis-à-vis India.

Jing-dong Yuan, a Chinese analyst, has identified four other issues that could seriously affect Sino–Indian relations and regional security.[74] These are: an Indian military strategy of 'regional deterrence' that seeks to consolidate its predominance in South Asia; a comprehensive defence modernization drive by New Delhi; an improving Indo–US relationship that could be used as a potential counterweight, if not a part of a containment strategy, against China; and India's post-Pokhran II diplomacy of engagement and entente with countries beyond New Delhi's traditional strategic domain—Japan, Vietnam, and, in a broader context, members of Association of South East Asian Nations (ASEAN), many of which have ongoing disputes with China.

However, notwithstanding these problems, the Chinese do not see India as their primary threat as their concerns are wider and for them an actual nuclear confrontation between the two Asian giants in the near future remains highly unlikely.

India, however, sees China as its primary security threat. There are several reasons for this. First, India suffered a major military

[71] Jing-dong Yuan, 'India's Rise After Pokhran II: Chinese Analyses and Assessments', *Asian Survey*, vol. XLI, no. 6, November–December 2001, p. 994.

[72] Zhang, op. cit., n. 68 above, p. 17.

[73] Yuan, op. cit., n. 71 above, p. 996

[74] Ibid.

defeat in the 1962 border war with China,[75] and it fears further Chinese intransigence on other territorial claims. China still occupies 38,000 sq. km. of Kashmir and claims another 90,000 sq. km. in the Indian state of Arunachal Pradesh. In addition, it has acquired 5,180 sq. km. territory of POK under the so-called Sino-Pakistan Boundary Agreement of 1963, which is still disputed.[76] Despite the Border Peace and Tranquillity Agreement of 1993, the Confidence Building Measures agreed upon in 1996,[77] and the boundary talks between the two for more than two decades, the two countries have so far not been able to solve their vexed territorial dispute.

Second, China's role in the proliferation of nuclear weapons to Pakistan in the 1980s and missile technology in the 1990s have been at the centre of India's immediate security concerns. Beijing has actively helped Islamabad by providing it with a tested design of a nuclear warhead, M-9 and M-11 ballistic missiles and missile components, fissile material, nuclear plants and ring magnets for enriched uranium.[78] These transfers led the US to impose sanctions against China twice, in 1991 and 1993. For years, India has been protesting against China's WMD transfers to Pakistan. But Beijing has rejected New Delhi's complaints either on the ground that it is within the bounds of treaty commitments, or flatly denied such collaboration with Islamabad. More recently, it made it clear that it would proliferate both vertically and horizontally if the US were to go ahead with the deployment of the National Missile Defense.

Third, India is no less concerned about the threat from Chinese

[75] For a comprehensive and dispassionate account of the precipitants of the Sino–Indian border war, see Stephen Hoffman, *India and the China Crisis*, Berkeley: University of California Press, 1990.

[76] India's Minister of State for External Affairs Digvijay Singh's statement in the Lok Sabha on 30 July 2003, quoted in 'China Illegally Claiming 90,000 sq. km. in Arunachal', *Hindu*, 31 July 2003.

[77] For details of these agreements, see Dipankar Banerji, ed., *CBMs in South Asia, Potential and Possibilities*, Colombo: RCSS, 2000, Appendix B, pp. 71–73, and Appendix C, pp. 74–80.

[78] Upendra Choudhury, 'China Has a Role', *Newstime*, 27 June 2002.

nuclear weapons.[79] (1) China's nuclear and delivery capabilities are several times bigger and better than those of India. (2) It is known that China is seriously engaged in efforts at modernizing its nuclear forces, aimed at cutting the military's size while qualitatively improving its weapons systems. China's nuclear and missile modernization programmes will likely assume greater importance, with emphasis on survivability of strategic nuclear warheads and the ability for escalation dominance in regional conflicts. (3) China has deployed a large number of medium- and short-range nuclear-tipped missiles and nuclear capable aircraft in Tibet.[80] It can be mentioned that at 4,000 metres above sea level and facing down on India, the Tibetan plateau is ideal for weapons deployment. As China has already signed an NFU agreement with Russia and a de-targeting agreement with the US, it is not clear whom these nuclear weapons are targeted at or intend to be targeted at. (4) China has lately added several conditions and changes to its NFU doctrine. One is that China's military planners do not consider the use of nuclear weapons on their own territory as a violation of their NFU doctrine.[81] This creates apprehension in India because China still officially claims the entire state of Arunachal Pradesh besides occupying a very large part of north-east Ladakh (the Kuen Lun, the Aksai Chin plateau and the Korakoram ranges) that India claims as its own. The other is that Beijing's nuclear doctrine has gradually shifted from minimum deterrence to limited deterrence, which connotes the capacity to use nuclear weapons for calibrated escalation and war fighting.[82]

[79] For a discussion of Indian misgivings about Chinese nuclear capabilities, see G.G. Mirchandani, *India's Nuclear Dilemma*, New Delhi: Popular Book Services, 1968.

[80] For a detailed account of China's missile deployment in Tibet, see W.P.S. Sidhu, 'India's Security and Nuclear Risk Reduction Measures', in *Nuclear Risk Reduction in South Asia*, ed. Michael Krepon and Michael Newbil, Washington, DC: Stimson Center, November 1998, pp. 21–4, at: http://www.stimson.org/pubs/cbm/sa/sidhufnl.pdf

[81] Swaran Singh, 'China's Nuclear Weapons and Doctrine', in *Nuclear India*, ed. Jasjit Singh, New Delhi: Knowledge World, in association with IDSA, 1998, p. 152.

[82] Andrew C. Winner and Toshi Yoshihara, *Nuclear Stability in South Asia*, Institute for Foreign Policy Analysis, Spring 2002, at: http://www.ifpa.org/pdf/nssa.pdf

Fourth, many Indians are worried that despite India's self-proclaimed declaration as a NWS, China knows that New Delhi has a long way to go before acquiring a credible and operational nuclear deterrent. Therefore, it is engaged in creating new hurdles with a view to freezing Indian capability at a point short of weaponization and deployment. For instance, at the Geneva CTBT negotiations in 1996, China insisted on the insertion of a controversial Entry-Into-Force (EIF) clause, which was strongly opposed by India.[83] The EIF stipulated that 'all nuclear capable states must sign the CTBT before it takes effect'.

Last, China has pursued a policy of 'containment of India and encirclement by proxy'. Besides Pakistan, it has armed all the countries bordering India. Indeed, some 90 per cent of China's arms sales go to India's neighbours.[84] It has taken advantage of Myanmar's isolation and provided $2 billion in military aid to that country.[85] It has established electronic listening posts on Myanmar's Coco Islands, opposite India's Andaman and Nicobar Islands, to monitor Indian naval activity and missile testing.

How does India intend to neutralize the Chinese threat? In three ways. First, India is developing a 3,000 km. China-specific ballistic missile called Agni-3.[86] This missile is slated for testing in 2005. Once Agni-3 is inducted, a major step towards deterrence stability vis-à-vis China will be achieved. The second is the development of a submarine based deterrent. India is working on a nuclear submarine project based on a Charlie-I class Russian submarine that is scheduled for completion in 2008–9.[87] Like their Western counterparts, many Indians argue that submarine-

[83] Mohan Malik, 'Nuclear Proliferation in Asia: The China Factor', *Australian Journal of International Affairs*, vol. 53, no. 1, 1999, p. 33.

[84] Ibid.

[85] Ibid.

[86] For more, see Upendra Choudhury, 'Dealing With the Danger of Ballistic Missiles in South Asia', paper presented at the Graduate Conference on Amity and Enmity: Patterns of Peace, War and Insecurity in the 21st Century, Department of Politics and International Relations, Cartmel College, Lancaster University, Lancaster, England, 18 April 2002, at: http://www.ceip.crg/files/projects/npp/pdf/SABM.pdf; and *Times of India*, 6 May 1999.

[87] Praveen Swami, 'Nuclear Submarine Project May Get a Kick-Start', *Hindu*, 27 May 2004.

based warheads are least vulnerable to a disarming first-strike.[88] Last, there are reports that India is soon going to have a missile defence capability.[89] It may either purchase the Arrow ABM systems from Israel or the Patriot-2 system from the US. Indian analysts argue that such a capability would enhance the uncertainty of its potential adversaries and act as a disincentive to their ready resort to nuclear weapons.[90] While there is unanimity among Indian strategic experts that India should retaliate mainly against the large population and industrial centres of China to obtain maximum pay-offs with its small nuclear force if that country goes for a nuclear first-strike,[91] they are divided on which Chinese cities should be targeted. While some feel that there is a need to target Beijing specifically, others do not see this as a necessary requirement.[92]

However, some points need to be mentioned in this context. First, India has not expressed an interest in catching up with China and is unlikely to seek more than a minimum deterrence capability against Beijing. Second, the push for a China-specific deterrent is not characterized by a sense of urgency because India does not see an imminent threat from that country.

While Indian experts consider China as India's primary security threat and are unanimous that New Delhi should take all necessary steps to have a credible minimum nuclear deterrent capability against 'the possibilities of a belligerent China',[93] they are divided

[88] For instance, see Vijay Sakhuja, 'Sea-Based Deterrence and Indian Security', *Strategic Analysis*, vol. XXV, no. 1, April 2001, pp. 21–32.

[89] 'Team on Missile Briefing', *Indian Express*, 17 February 2005.

[90] See for instance, Mohan, op. cit., n. 32 above.

[91] Gurmeet Kanwal, 'A Nuclear Targeting Philosophy for India', *Strategic Analysis*, vol. 24, no. 3, June 2000, pp. 459–74.

[92] For an insightful discussion on divergences, see K. Subrahmanyam, 'A Credible Nuclear Deterrent: Logic of the Nuclear Doctrine', *Times of India*, 4 October 1999; Vijay K. Nair, *Nuclear India*, New Delhi: Lancer International, 1992, pp. 133–51; Ashley Tellis, 'Towards a Force-in-Being: The Logic, Structure and Utility of India's Emerging Nuclear Posture', *Strategic Studies* (special issue), 'India as an Emerging Power', vol. 25, no. 4, 2003; and General K. Sundarji, 'Imperatives of Indian Minimum Nuclear Deterrence', *Agni*, vol. 2, no. 1, May 1996.

[93] Amitabh Mattoo, 'India's Nuclear Policy in an Anarchic World', in his *India's Nuclear Deterrence Pokhran II and Beyond* (ed.), New Delhi: Har-Anand Publishers, 1998, pp. 18–19.

on the outbreak of a full-scale war between the two countries. However, for many, a limited border war between India and China cannot be entirely ruled out in future.[94] One analyst mentions at least two scenarios in which China could indulge in a limited war with India.[95] The first one lies five to ten years from now when China has attained a potent conventional capability to project itself under a nuclear deterrence umbrella and decides to flex its muscles in order to seek a solution to its claims in Arunachal Pradesh. The second scnenario may unfold if the ruling Communist Party of China feels threatened, and to divert attention from domestic politics, decides to 'teach India a lesson'. According to him, for China to find a reason would not be difficult. One plausible excuse could be the blame China attaches to India for provoking a nuclear arms race in South Asia. Many others warn that China is still to demonstrate its commitment to non-violent resolution of disputes, and that, in turn, reflects a proclivity for the use of force, which may be constrained only temporarily by the exigencies of current economic policies.[96]

While many do not rule out a future limited border war with China, there is general agreement that Beijing would actually not use nuclear weapons against New Delhi in a 'bolt-from-the-blue' first-strike. K. Subrahmanyam argues that the threats from China will be 'more in the nature of nuclear blackmail than of actual use and the extreme case will be the use of a few weapons'.[97]

The point, however, is that if there is a limited war between

[94] Gurmeet Kanwal, 'Does India Need Tactical Weapons', *Strategic Analysis*, vol. XXIV, no 3, June 2000, pp. 247–64; and A. K. Sachdev, 'India's Surface-to-Surface Missiles', *Strategic Analysis*, vol. XXIV, no. 2, May 2000, pp. 265–82.

[95] A.K. Sachdev 'Chinese Missiles: Winning the Limited War', *Strategic Analysis*, vol. XXIV, no. 3, June 2000, p. 536.

[96] Rajesh M. Basrur, 'India's Escalation-Resistant Nuclear Posture' in *Escalation Control and the Nuclear Option in South Asia*, ed. Michael Krepon, Rodney W. Jones and Ziad Haider, Washington, DC: Stimson Center, 2004, pp. 1–19, at: http://www.stimson.org/southasia/pdf/ESCCONTROLCHAPTER3.pdf

[97] K. Subrahmanyam, 'Nuclear Force Design and Minimum Deterrence Strategy for India', in *Future Imperiled: India's Security in the 1990's and Beyond*, ed. Bharat Karnad, New Delhi: Viking Penguin, 1994, p. 177.

India and China or a nuclear stand-off between the two, there could be risks of intentional, accidental, or unauthorized use of nuclear weapons as discussed in the Indo–Pakistani crisis situation. After all, the Chinese nuclear arsenal lacks sufficient technological barriers to inadvertent, accidental, or unauthorized use as these are widely dispersed; Permissive Action Links (PALs)—these are electronic circuits wired into a bomb and do not allow activation except under very particular circumstances—are not installed in them.[98] The Chinese, like Indians, have, no doubt, adopted organizational alternatives to technological safety features—establishing a nuclear control organization independent of the strategic delivery forces, in addition to keeping warheads removed from their delivery vehicles.[99] The problem is that when successive governments cannot guarantee regime stability, there are questions with regard to ensuring the organization's constant loyalty to the autho-rized decision makers.[100] This is a legitimate concern for a totalitarian country like China.

[98] Dan Caldwell, 'PLAs: A Description and Proposal', *Survival*, May–June 1987, p. 231.

[99] Robert E. Rehbein, 'Managing Proliferation in South Asia: A Case for Assistance to Unsafe Nuclear Arsenals', *Non-Proliferation Review*, vol. 9, no. 1, Spring 2002, p. 97.

[100] Ibid.

CHAPTER 3

Nuclear Risks Reduction Measures in South Asia

Since India perceives significant nuclear threats from China, it may not negotiate any credible nuclear risk reduction measure with Pakistan unless Beijing is brought into the fold. Moreover, many Indians consider China as an extension of the Pakistani nuclear dimension.[1] To quote one analyst, 'India would have to negotiate not only with Pakistan, which is merely a recipient of the long-range nuclear capable missiles, but also China, which is the primary supplier.'[2] They, therefore, advocate China's inclusion in any nuclear risk reduction dialogue in South Asia.

The introduction of China as a key player in the South Asian nuclear chessboard means that NRRMs, in order to be more credible, should be trilateral in nature. But under the present circumstances, as we will see later, bilateral risk reduction between India and Pakistan and India and China holds more promise than a trilateral framework. These are discussed below.

Nuclear Risk Reduction Measures Between India and Pakistan

My discussion of nuclear risks in the Indo–Pakistani situation makes it clear that, given the possibility of a conventional war escalating into a nuclear exchange, nuclear risks between India and Pakistan cannot be addressed by nuclear-specific measures

[1] See, for instance, Manpreet Sethi, 'Dangers from WMD: Any Different in South Asia'?, *Strategic Analysis*, vol. XXIV, no. 11, February 2001, pp. 1989–2004.

[2] W.P.S. Sidhu, 'India's Security and Nuclear Risk Reduction Measures', in *Nuclear Risk Reduction in South Asia*, ed. Michael Krepon and Michael Newbil, Washington, DC: Stimson Center, November 1998, p. 28, at: htpp://www.stimson.org/pubs/cbm/sa/sidhufnl.pdf

alone. While the nuclear measures are useful in their own way, it is even more important to consider mechanisms that reduce the prospects for conventional military tensions between Indian and Pakistan. In other words, the challenge before New Delhi and Islamabad lies in preventing not just a nuclear conflict, but in minimizing all military tensions.[3] This can be done in four ways: dismantling the infrastructure of terrorism by Pakistan; abandoning the limited war doctrine by India; strengthening the existing conventional Confidence Building Measures (CBM) and negotiating new ones; and finding a just and permanent solution to the Kashmir dispute.

Pakistan's commitment to end terrorist violence against India is necessary to reduce tension between the two countries. Islamabad should end support for militants, prevent infiltration across the LOC, dismantle terrorist training camps, and take other steps to crack down on the terrorists. The attack on the Indian Parliament in December 2001 clearly indicates that as long as terrorist strikes continue, there can always be situations which demand escalation of conventional military conflict with all its attendant risks. And democracies would be under greater pressure in these circumstances as the case of the USA in the post-9/11 period shows. Moreover, Pakistan needs to take a lesson from its strategic ally, China, which stopped its 20-year-old support to the Naga insurgency within months of India's nuclear test of 1974.[4]

Dismantling the infrastructure of terrorism by Pakistan is not, however, a favour to India. It will be equally beneficial to Pakistan. No one can brush aside the fact that Pakistan's Afghan policy took it to the brink of disaster and its support for terrorism in Afghanistan and Kashmir has fuelled destabilizing domestic extremism.[5] Moreover, Pakistani support to terrorism has severely undermined its international image. Now, it is increasingly recognized as the 'epicentre' of international terrorism.[6]

[3] C. Raja Mohan, 'Beyond Nuclear Stability', *Hindu*, 22 June 2004.

[4] Jasjit Singh, 'Talking Points, Sticky Issues', *Indian Express*, 9 April 2004.

[5] For more about the fallouts of domestic terrorism, see Vijay Oberoi, 'Indo-Pak Search for Peace', *Tribune*, 4 October 2003.

[6] President Musharraf, for example, while addressing a government-sponsored

Similarly, Pakistan's policy on terrorism has undermined its economy, increased its diplomatic isolation, and made its close friends such as the US and China to behave unpredictably. Once Afghanistan is stabilized and the Al-Qaida mopped up, the Americans will not show any real interest in South Asia. The once reliable China, alarmed at Pakistan's support for Uighur Islamic radicals, is moving towards an understanding with India over its border dispute.[7]

Thus, it is for Pakistan to decide if the game is worth the risks. But Islamabad should remain under no illusion that it can obtain an advantageous outcome of the Kashmir issue through its cross-border terrorism against India. Such a dangerous policy has only made the problem more intractable. To quote Ayaz Amir, a respected Pakistani columnist, 'We have tried changing the status quo in Kashmir from the first shots fired in 1947 right down to the Kargil adventure of 1999. We have only succeeded in making it more permanent.'[8]

India should similarly realize that its new military doctrine to fight a limited war under nuclear conditions is not a viable option against Pakistan. Even the troop mobilization against Pakistan in 2001–2 resulted in a nine-month stalemate because of the nuclear factor. Moreover, India does not have the overwhelming military superiority over Pakistan required to score a decisive victory in the short run. Therefore, the most likely scenario is that India will get bogged down in a war, and outside powers will intervene and bring the matter to the UN Security Council, which will

---

ulema and *mashaika* convention, focussed on 'the four dangerous perceptions' prevailing about the country in the world community. He observed that Pakistan could suffer economically and face UN sanctions if these impressions were not removed. He identified sectarianism, nuclear proliferation, the terrorist activities in Afghanistan and those in Kashmir from the soil of Pakistan as challenges. He further declared, 'What kind of a country is ours where everyone incites people to take arms in the name of jihad? This is not jihad.'

[7] Stephen Philip Cohen, 'Nuclear Weapons and Nuclear War in South Asia: An Unknowable Future', paper presented to the UN University Conference on South Asia, Tokyo, May 2002, at: http://www.brook.edu/dybdocroot/views/speeches/cohens20020501.pdf

[8] Ayaz Amir, 'The Middle Path to Peace', *Indian Express*, 14 May 2003.

enforce a ceasefire.[9] Further, India cannot see the problem of terrorism in Kashmir in military terms alone. It needs a political approach as well. Finally, India cannot emerge as a truly great Asian country if it is bogged down by the Kashmir conflict and if Pakistan remains openly hostile to it.[10] Therefore, as war or proxy war are associated with nuclear risks and neither side has been able to achieve its objective for such a long time, it would be logical to rethink the basic approaches. In other words, it is time the two countries moved towards mutually negotiated conventional CBMs to reduce the prospect of any substantive advantage through conventional military offensive. Many models, like the Conventional Forces in Europe Treaty, exist.[11]

However, given the institutionalized distrust between the two countries, grandiose declarations and unrealistic proposals are bound to fail. As C. Raja Mohan rightly remarks, 'India and Pakistan must learn to walk before they want to run.'[12]

India and Pakistan could consider a range of simple ideas. These include: institutionalized contacts between the two military establishments at various levels from the headquarters down to the field commanders across the border; better communication links; exchange of military delegations; better methods of crisis management, etc.

Besides, they could also strengthen the CBMs that already exist between the two countries. These include a notification of Army exercises of a certain size near the border,[13] and a commitment by the two Air Forces not to violate each other's airspaces.[14] Although

[9] Muchkund Dubey, 'The Missing Options', *Hindu*, 4 June 2002.

[10] Victor M. Gobarev, 'India as a World Power', *Policy Analysis*, 11 September 2000, at: http://www.cato.org/pubs/pas/pa-38/es.pdf

[11] For a detailed overview of the treaty provisions, see: http://www1.umn.edu/humanrts/peace/docs/conweaeurope.html

[12] Mohan, op. cit., n. 3 above.

[13] For more, see 'India–Pakistan Agreement on Advance Notice on Military Exercises, Manoeuvres and Troop Movements, 6 April 1991', *Strategic Digest*, vol. 34, no. 6, June 2004, pp. 870–72.

[14] For details, see 'India–Pakistan Agreement on Prevention of Air Space Violations and for Permitting Over-Flights and Landings by Military Aircraft, 6 April 1991', at: http://meadev.nic.in/Opn/kargil/air_agreement.htm

these two agreements were signed in 1991, their implementation has been less than satisfactory because there has been no real political acceptance of these CBMs in either India or Pakistan. Moreover, neither side has been willing to underline the importance of avoiding conventional military conflicts.

Success in this direction would lead to mutual security at lower costs for both states. More important, the process itself would help to reduce threat perceptions and also hold a promise of stability in relations that is the bedrock of nuclear risk reduction. It is important to mention here that an expert-level meeting on conventional CBMs between India and Pakistan was held in Islamabad in December 2004. The two sides held discussions on the significance of and overall approaches to conventional CBMs and exchanged views on various proposals.[15] On conventional weapons, India has proposed an agreement to maintain a ceasefire along the LOC in Kashmir and more military contacts.[16]

Certainly, it is highly desirable for both India and Pakistan to redouble their efforts to find a reasonable solution of the Kashmir issue in a violence-free environment. But since it is a very complex issue and cannot be solved overnight, both New Delhi and Islamabad should focus their attention on the nuclear risk reduction issue that is extremely vital in view of the horrendous stakes involved. Both should realize that in a nuclear relationship, nothing is more vital than the necessity of preventing war and nuclear catastrophe. India and Pakistan have to arrive at an understanding that although Kashmir might be central to their respective identities as nations, avoiding nuclear conflict comes first.[17] This means separating the dispute over Kashmir from the larger nuclear relationship so as to maintain a broad stability in the way that India and China have done. Before discussing various risk reduc-

[15] For more, see 'Joint Statement, India–Pakistan Expert-Level Meeting on Conventional CBMs, Islamabad, 15 December 2004', at: http://www.indianembassy.ru/docs-htm/en/en_05_04_t2412_2004.htm

[16] 'India–Pak End Second Round of Nuke CBMs Talks', ANI, at: http://athens-olympics-2004.newkerala.com/?action=fullnews&id=48024

[17] Rajesh Basrur, 'Nuclear India at the Crossroads, *Arms Control Today*, vol. 33, no. 7, September 2003, p. 9.

tion measures, it is necessary to discuss the history of risk reduction measures between India and Pakistan ever since they nuclearized.

History

In the past, nuclear discourse between India and Pakistan tended to be adversarial and propagandist. Pakistan saw India's proposals on global disarmament as rhetoric aimed at avoiding regional imperatives. India, on the other hand, saw Pakistani proposals for regional arms control as designed to limit India's nuclear options and shift the focus to Kashmir. This resulted in lack of nuclear CBMs between India and Pakistan, except the one signed between Prime Minister Rajiv Gandhi and his Pakistani counterpart Benazir Bhutto in 1988. Under this agreement, India and Pakistan declared that they would not attack each other's nuclear facilities.[18]

However, the incremental evolution of their attitudes during the 1990s, the intense exposure of the Indian strategic community to the unending Track-II initiatives from the US, their open nuclear tests in May 1998, and the fear of the international community of South Asia becoming a nuclear flashpoint, all contributed to the new Indian and Pakistani support to arms control and nuclear CBMs. Accordingly, the first formal discussion on nuclear and conventional CBMs was held between their foreign secretaries in October 1998.[19] This was further consolidated in the MoU on

[18] For more, see 'Agreement Between India and Pakistan on Prohibition of Attack Against Nuclear Installations and Facilities, 31 December 1998', at: http://www.indian embassy.org/South_Asia/pakistan/Prohibition_Attack_ Nuclear_Dec_31

[19] During the foreign secretary-level talks in October 1998, India had proposed the extension of the hotline between the Director General Military Operation (DGMOs), revival of the hotline between the foreign secretaries, extension of the existing arrangement on non-attack on nuclear installations close to population and economic centres, an increase in information exchange in the nuclear field to facilitate greater transparency, and the setting up of a consultative machinery to review and implement CBMs. Pakistan presented its proposal for a Strategic Restraint Regime in South Asia. As part of this regime, it had called for the prevention of a nuclear and missile race, an agreement on risk reduction measures, non-induction of air-based and sea-based missile systems, and a nuclear doctrine of minimum deterrence capability. On the conventional front, Islamabad had suggested a mutual and balanced

CBMs that the foreign secretaries of India and Pakistan signed during Prime Minister Vajpayee's Lahore visit in February 1999.[20] The Kargil War in mid-1999 and the subsequent military coup in Pakistan, however, resulted in a complete absence of dialogue between India and Pakistan. India insisted that it could not hold a dialogue with Pakistan until the latter ceased support for the insurgents in Kashmir. Pakistan, on the contrary, insisted that it would be ready to start a dialogue with India only when the 'core' issue of Kashmir was on the negotiating table. These two antithetical positions have contributed to a political deadlock.

However, the absence of inter-governmental dialogue did not deter the security experts of both countries consisting of retired foreign secretaries, generals, admirals, and diplomats to meet frequently at the Track-II level to address the nuclear issues between India and Pakistan. The dialogue was started after a mutual understanding that the subject be discussed outside the ambit of issues and conflicts affecting relations between New Delhi and Islamabad.[21] These were needed to ensure progress on nuclear issues by isolating it from other complex issues. The Indian side was led by the Delhi Policy Group (DPG), and the Pakistani experts

---

reduction of forces and armament levels. These proposals did not materialize because of the Pakistani attempt to link the nuclear issue with the Kashmir question, and India's argument that its defence preparedness was not oriented to the threat from within the region alone: Amit Barua, 'India–Pakistan Begin Talks on Nuclear CBMs', *Hindu*, 20 June 2004.

[20] In the Lahore MoU of February 1999, India and Pakistan acknowledged that:

The nuclear dimension of the security environment of the two countries adds to their responsibility for avoidance of conflict between the two countries' and that they were 'Convinced of the importance of mutually agreed CBMs for improving the security situation'. Among other efforts, they committed themselves to 'take immediate steps for reducing the risk of accidental or unauthorized use of nuclear weapons and discuss the concepts and doctrines with a view to elaborating measures for confidence building in the nuclear and conventional fields, aimed at prevention of conflict. (For more, see: http://www.indianembassy.org/South_Asia/Pakistan/lahoredeclaration.html)

[21] V.R. Raghavan, 'Nuclear Dialogue With Pakistan', *Hindu*, 25 January 2001.

met under the aegis of the Islamabad Policy Research Institute (IPRI).[22]

The DPG and the IPRI had held two meetings in 2000 on the subject of nuclear risk reduction. These proved fruitful in improving understanding and laying the groundwork for continuing the dialogue. A third meeting was held between the two in Islamabad in January 2001. This meeting was structured on specific issues related to NRRMs.[23] The Delhi Policy Group had also launched a Nuclear Policy Stewardship project to educate the public and authorities about nuclear risk management.

Although the Track-II dialogue did not accomplish much due to a number of reasons,[24] yet it certainly provided the opportunity to examine ways to reduce nuclear risks and prepared the ground for future inter-governmental dialogue on the issue.

However, the real breakthrough came during the 12th South Asian Association for Regional Cooperation (SAARC) summit in Islamabad in January 2004 when Vajpayee and Musharraf prepared the framework of contacts between the two countries that was suspended following the crisis in 2001–2.

Following this, the Indo–Pak expert-level talks on nuclear CBMs was held in New Delhi in June 2004.[25] After two days of talks, the two countries came together for the first time to state that their nuclear weapons were instruments of stability. They also announced a set of CBMs on nuclear weapons. These included their decision to persist with the moratorium on nuclear weapons testing until 'extraordinary events jeopardise their supreme

[22] 'Dialogue Will Reduce Threat of Nuclear War', *Hindustan Times*, 17 January 2001.

[23] 'Accord on Nuclear Risk Reduction', *Hindu*, 17 January 2001.

[24] According to Raja Menon, the Track-II dialogue did not materialize because of the indifferent attitude of the GoI, specially the Ministry of External Affairs, as it wanted not to be infected by the Track-II movement, which it suspected was run by a 'foreign hand': Raja Menon, 'Nuclear CBMs, Seriously', *Indian Express*, 24 June 2004.

[25] 'India–Pakistan Begin Talks on Nuclear CBMs', *Hindu*, 20 June 2004. Also see 'India, Pakistan Agree on Hotline Between Foreign Secretaries', *Hindu*, 21 June 2004.

interests', setting up a hotline between their foreign secretaries, and upgradation of the existing communication links between their directors general of military operations. Both sides also agreed that they would try to reach an accord with technical parameters on pre-notification of missile test flight. The two states also called for a dialogue with acknowledged nuclear countries that include the five permanent members of the UN Security Council and demanded that they should discuss ways to reduce the risks from nuclear weapons.[26] In order to operationalize the 20 June statement, both India and Pakistan met again on 14–15 December in Islamabad for the Second Round of Nuclear CBMs between the two countries. They zeroed in on formalization of pre-notification of missile flight testing and effective communication between the two countries to prevent misunderstandings and reduce nuclear related risks. Both sides also 'reiterated their desire to move the process of nuclear CBMs forward'.[27] The Third Round of Nuclear CBMs between India and Pakistan was held in New Delhi on 4–5 August 2005. Both sides committed 'to pre-notify in a structured format flight testing of ballistic missiles, with the objective of enhancing mutual confidence and engendering predictability and transparency of intent'. The two nuclear weapon states also agreed to establish a hotline link between their foreign secretaries to avert misunderstandings and reduce risks of a nuclear emergency. Both countries also discussed 'in a cordial and constructive atmosphere' their respective security concepts and nuclear doctrines to make the region safe from an accidental nuclear disaster.

A close look at these three rounds of nuclear talks between India and Pakistan shows that there has not been any substantial progress on any nuclear CBMs discussed so far. Both the countries, on the contrary, have evaded the 'core points' set out in Lahore in

[26] 'Joint Statement, India–Pakistan Expert-Level Meeting on Nuclear CBMs, Islamabad, 15 December 2004', at: http://www.indianembassy.ru/docs-htm/en/en_05_04_t2412_2004.htm

[27] Subhas Kapila, 'Pakistan Evades Core Issues in Nuclear CBMs Talks with India', South Asian Analysis Group, at: http://www.saag.org/papers11/paper1041.html

the MoU in February 1999. These core points are: (1) Nuclear Doctrine and Security Concepts; (2) Commitment to Undertake National Measures to Reducing Risk of Accidental or Unauthorized Use of Nuclear Weapons; and (3) Consultative Mechanism for Implementing Review. It could be argued that a dialogue on nuclear CBMs has commenced between India and Pakistan, and that itself is a big achievement.[28] But this consolation is not enough. There are several reasons why the nuclear dialogue has not made any significant progress. First, both sides have a critical problem of 'mutual trust and faith' and are wary of each other's intentions and commitments. Second, Pakistan links the progress in any field with the 'progress on Kashmir'. Both India and Pakistan should shed their negative attitude towards each other. Pakistan should also drop its insistence that issues such as the future of Kashmir should be addressed with urgency. In order to claim themselves as being truly mature and responsible NWS, both countries need to work hard for concrete outcomes from their ongoing dialogue process and focus on the following risk reduction measures to reduce the risks of intentional, accidental, or unauthorized use of nuclear weapons in South Asia.

These NRRMs could be undertaken both unilaterally and bilaterally. The unilateral measures are discussed as under.

Unilateral Risk Reduction Measures

Unilaterally, both countries could undertake steps to upgrade the physical security and safety of their atomic installations. Nuclear facilities should have barriers such as fences, vehicle traps and pop-up crash barriers to prevent suicidal truck-bomb attacks. These can be augmented by the presence of security guards, surveillance cameras, motion detection sensors and a system of identification for authorized persons and vehicles. Protection forces of plants should have sharpshooters to prevent extremists armed

[28] For more, see 'India–Pakistan Joint Statement on Nuclear Talks', *Indian Express*, 21 June 2004; and John Cherian, 'Building Confidence', *Frontline*, vol. 33, no. 7, 16 July 2004, pp. 44–5.

with sophisticated weapons from gaining entry or firing a rocket from outside. The reliability of nuclear plant employees should be periodically reviewed by intelligence agencies. It should be ensured that only responsible people are involved in nuclear weapons management. Such personnel should be 'highly aware of the horrific nature of nuclear weapons, not be prone to knee jerk responses and remain extremely disciplined',[29] even under adverse circumstances. This is necessary to deter 'insider' links with terrorist elements.

Nuclear materials also need extraordinary security precautions. Weapons-usable materials should be protected in the same manner as nuclear bombs. Even small quantities of these materials should be transported only under heavy guard. India and Pakistan should establish Nuclear Emergency Search Teams (NEST) on the US pattern to find and render harmless stolen nuclear weapons, improvised nuclear devices or weapons-useable materials. India should ratify the Convention on Nuclear Safety.[30]

[29] Feroz Hassan Khan, 'Challenges to Nuclear Stability in South Asia', *Non-Proliferation Review*, vol. 10, no. 1, Spring 2003, p. 72.

[30] According to press reports, Pakistan has introduced a Bill named 'Export Control on Goods, Technologies, Material and Equipment Related to Nuclear and Biological Weapons and Their Delivery Systems Act, 2004' in Parliament to punish nuclear proliferation. As per the proposed Bill, a violation of the ban on the export of any material or technology related to nuclear and chemical weapons will be punishable with up to fourteen years in prison, a fine up to Rs. 5 million ($85,000), and forfeiture of a convict's property and assets: 'Pakistan Moves to Punish Nuclear Proliferation', *Hindu*, 9 June 2004. It is a party to Early Notification of Nuclear Accidents and on the Convention on the Physical Protection of Nuclear Weapons. For more, see Garima Singh, 'Pakistan's Nuclear Safety Bill', at: http://www.ipcs.org/Nuclear_articles2.jsp?action=showview&kValue=1561&issue=1015&status=article&mod=a; and Zafar Nawaz Jaspal, 'Safety and Security of Pakistan Nuclear Capabilities', *IPRI Journal*, vol. 2, no. 1, Winter 2002, at: http://www.ipri-pak.org/winterjournal02/safetyandsecurity.htm

Similarly, India has recently passed the Weapons of Mass Destruction and their Delivery System (Prohibition of Unlawful Activities) Bill, 2005. The Bill seeks to prevent transfer of weapons of mass destruction and their technology from India and to prohibit individuals from dealing with WMDs in any form, including manufacturing, transporting, possessing, exporting and brokering. The punishment for manufacturing WMDs or abetting terrorists is a minimum jail term of five

Both India and Pakistan should sign the additional protocol to the NPT.[31] This may be difficult at the moment because both New Delhi and Islamabad have refused to sign the NPT, as it does not recognize their new nuclear status. It is my contention that the NPT is not a 'sacred cow'. It should be amended wherever necessary. The international context has changed so much, thanks to the rise of non-state actors such as terrorist groups, suicide attacks, new incentives for proliferation of WMD, and failing states. Amendment of the NPT has also become inevitable as a result of the accumulated failures over the last three and a half decades. Almost every one of its articles has been violated with impunity. Therefore, the NPT should be modernized in the light of the recent challenges and be made more realistic by accommodating India, Pakistan (and Israel) into its fold.

Both India and Pakistan should use PAL devices in their nuclear weapons to render stolen arms useless.[32] Similarly, surveillance techniques like ground-based monitoring, overhead remote sensing, and video cameras with thermal imaging should be used

---

years, which may extend to life imprisonment, besides being liable to fine. The first conviction for unauthorized export of WMDs is a fine of Rs. 3 lakh to Rs. 20 lakh and the second sentence will attract imprisonment for six months to five years, besides fine. Subsequent offences will lead to jail terms of one to seven years. The fine for using or making false documents is Rs. 5 lakh or five times the cost of the material or service, whichever is more. Any individual contravening a provision for which no specific punishment has been specified shall be punishable for a maximum of one year in prison, or fine, or both. In case of an offence committed by a company, persons involved in the offence will be prosecuted. The Bill also provides for appointment of advisory committees and an appellate authority. For more, see 'Weapons of Mass Destruction Bill', *Hindu*, 11 May 2005.

[31] The additional protocol to the NPT was established by the International Atomic Energy Agency (IAEA) in 1997. Its main aim is to allow the UN's nuclear watchdog to verify a country's declared nuclear activities and ensure the latter is not hiding material it could use to build a nuclear bomb. For more, see: http://www.spacewar.com/2003/031218114923.ghpco7d2.html

[32] A PAL is an electronic device that prevents arming the weapon unless the correct codes are used in it. For more, see Bruce G. Blair, *The Logic of Accidental Nuclear War*, Washington, DC: Brookings Institution, 1993; and Dan Caldwell, 'PLAs: A Description and Proposal', *Survival*, May–June 1987, pp. 224–38.

to reduce the danger of unauthorized release or movement of nuclear weapons. Both should also acquire the latest technologies for packaging, sealing and monitoring of fissile and radioactive materials, acquire updated equipment for real time communication among transport vehicles, escorts and a transportation operation centre, and establish an autonomous and highly trained security force for protecting nuclear facilities and materials instead of depending on a nationwide security agency that undertakes other assignments as well.

Some other unilateral measures for prevention of nuclear use could also be undertaken. First, use of nuclear alerts or threats of nuclear weapons use for political manoeming or intimidation should be scrupulously avoided. Second, both India and Pakistan should abstain from adoption of launch-on-warning systems or policies.[33] Third, both countries should reduce the vulnerability of their missiles and aircraft to pre-emptive attacks. Last, both New Delhi and Islamabad need to go beyond rhetorical commitment to non-proliferation towards the creation of more effective control over export of sensitive materials and technologies. This would involve the drafting of new laws as well as modernizing of their enforcement mechanisms in relation to non-proliferation.

Bilateral Risk Reduction Measures

Bilateral measures are divided into three main categories: Initial Steps, Medium-Term Steps, and Long-Term Steps. These are divided on the basis of whether they *do* or *do not* require a change in the nuclear strategy and posture between India and Pakistan. Moreover, the time required for their implementation also varies. However, most of these measures are multi-purpose in character, i.e. if implemented properly, they could reduce the risks of intentional, accidental, or unauthorized use of nuclear weapons. Therefore, they are not discussed separately.

[33] Susan M. Burns, 'Preventing Nuclear War: Arms Management', in Stephen Philip Cohen, ed., *Nuclear Proliferation in South Asia: The Prospects for Arms Control*, Boulder, CO: Westview Press, 1991, p. 109.

INITIAL STEPS

Although risk reduction measures are imperative, the suspicion, mistrust, and animosity between India and Pakistan mean that some of the most important measures would be certain to be non-starters. It would be best to concentrate first on measures that can be implemented without requiring any significant change in current Indo-Pakistan security policies. If these measures were implemented, they could lay the foundation for more significant measures at a later stage.

Reliable and Dedicated Communication: Given short flight times, and the potential for misinterpretation of data, it is vital for India and Pakistan to have a reliable, secure, dedicated, and fast system for communicating with each other. Both countries acknowledged the importance of communication in the MoU signed in Lahore 1999 and hotlines (direct communication links) exist between their heads of government, heads of military operations, and now between their foreign secretaries, but this means of communication has seldom been used during crisis.

India and Pakistan should pledge that whatever be the circumstances, they will use this link in a crisis. Moreover, they should also have hotlines for their Air Forces and nuclear establishments.[34]

Advance Notification of Missile and Space Launches: Although both India and Pakistan agreed at Lahore to 'provide each other with advance notification in respect of ballistic missiles flight tests',[35] and both sides now issue such notifications, there is no formal treaty between New Delhi and Islamabad to this effect. The agreement should be converted into a treaty, based on the provisions of the 1988 Ballistic Missile Launch Notification Agreement between

[34] Upendra Choudhury, 'Dealing With the Danger of Ballistic Missiles in South Asia', paper presented at the Graduate Conference on Amity and Enmity: Patterns of Peace, War and Insecurity in the 21st Century, organized by the Department of Politics and International Relations, Cartmel College, Lancaster University, Lancaster, England, 18 April 2002, at: http://www.ceip.org/files/projects/npp/pdf/SABM.pdf

[35] Lahore Declaration, op. cit., n. 18 above.

the US and the Soviet Union.[36] Notification should include planned launch date, launch area, and area of impact. Any postponement or cancellation should also be reported.

Moreover, other measures such as refraining from testing during periods of heightened crisis or tension, launching missile tests on trajectories away from adversaries, and joint monitoring of missile test sites could also lead to tension reduction.

Because of the overlap in the technology and physical characteristics between ballistic missiles and space launch vehicles, the two countries should also notify each other in the case of a space launch, with the same objective—to reduce the risk of nuclear war as a consequence of misinterpretation, miscalculation, or accident.[37]

Notification of Movement of Missile Forces: India and Pakistan should sign an agreement to notify each other about the movement or repositioning of missile forces, which would add to confidence building and minimize the chance that motives will be misinterpreted.

Both India and Pakistan could agree to notify each other of their missile alert status during times of crisis or war. Moreover, they could also notify the exercises that utilize nuclear capable forces or equipment.

MEDIUM-TERM STEPS

Once the Initial Steps build necessary confidence and trust between India and Pakistan, they could undertake Medium-Term Steps to reduce nuclear risks. These are discussed below.

Banning and Dismantling Conventional Missiles: Both India and Pakistan should ban and progressively dismantle a host of conventional warhead missiles that confuse the opposite side as 'nuclear missiles'. This confusion could dangerously lead to

[36] For more about this treaty, see Nazir Kamal and Pravin Sawhney, 'Missile Control in South Asia and the Role of Cooperative Monitoring Technology', CMC Occasional Paper, Appendix K, at: http://www.cmc.sandia.gov/Links/about/papers/SAND98-0505-4/index.html

[37] Upendra Choudhury, 'Too Close For Comfort', *Bulletin of Atomic Scientists*, vol. 59, no. 2, March–April 2003, p. 22.

misperception and possible use of nuclear weapons in a crisis.[38] These dangerous missiles include the Indian Prithvi and Pakistani Hatf-I, II, IIA and IIIA.

Joint Exercises to Study Potential Nuclear Accidents: New Delhi and Islamabad should undertake joint studies to reveal the potential for accident during nuclear operations. Similarly, both sides could stand to learn more about the weaknesses in their respective command, control and communication (C^3) arrangements and systems, and in particular both countries should compare and contrast their evolving C^3 systems to the Cold War history of technical errors and bureaucratic blunders that have surfaced in declassified US literature. Accidents can take place in any deterrent relationship, whatever the nature of nuclear strategies and deployment. These exercises could be undertaken unilaterally, but they are likely to reveal much more if they are at least partially bilateral in nature, because only truly international exercises can demonstrate the chances of mutual misperceptions.[39]

Establishing a South Asian Nuclear Risk Reduction Centre: To meet the objectives of the Lahore MoU, both India and Pakistan could establish a Nuclear Risk Reduction Centre (NRRC) to manage their nuclear affairs. Such a centre could be a clearing house for nuclear information and serve as a central point for data collection and dissemination.[40] A draft agreement prepared by a group of Indians, Pakistanis and Americans with the help of the Washington-based Centre for Strategic and International Studies has recommended the following functions for such a South Asian Centre.

- The NRRC will complement existing communication channels between India and Pakistan.
- Both sides will notify each other of activities or events on its territory that may be misperceived and lead to conflict.
- Exchange information that both sides are obliged to pass on under existing arrangements.

[38] Raja Menon, 'Nuclear CBMs, Seriously', *Indian Express*, 24 June 2004.

[39] Michael Ryn Kraig, 'The Political and Strategic Imperatives of Nuclear Deterrence in South Asia', *India Review*, vol. 2, no. 1, January 2003, p. 40.

[40] For more, see Rafi-uz Zaman Khan, 'Pakistan and India: Can NRRCs Help Strengthen Peace?', Stimson Center Occasional Paper no. 49, December 2002.

- Seek and receive clarifications on ambiguous events in each other's territory.[41]

Due to close geographical proximity and high population density, radiation hazard from nuclear accidents from one country to the other is quite possible. For this, both should establish a Disaster Monitoring System. Moreover, both countries should also work together to monitor the activities of transnational terrorist groups.

Non-Deployment of ABM and Early Warning Systems: Both countries should declare a moratorium on acquisition and deployment of ABM systems.[42] This would inject new instability and gravely undermine any nuclear restraint regime in the region.

Similarly, both India and Pakistan should stop installing early warning systems that clearly, in the specific South Asian context where the response time is dangerously short, increase the risk of accidental or unauthorized nuclear war.

LONG-TERM STEPS

If the Medium-Term Steps are successful and there is significant improvement in the Indo–Pakistani relationship across a broad front, both countries could go for more extensive steps that would drastically reduce nuclear risks in South Asia.

Small Nuclear Arsenals: Both India and Pakistan have declared a minimum nuclear deterrence posture.[43] But their deterrence requirement appears dynamic and there are no clear limits on weapons

[41] 'US Tip for CBMs: Nuclear Risk Centres', *Indian Express*, 8 August 2004.

[42] There are reports that India is attempting to purchase the Arrow ABM systems from Israel, which it is developing in collaboration with the US. While Washington is yet to clear the Arrow sale to New Delhi, it has offered to discuss the sale of its own Patriot-2 system to India. An American team even visited India in February 2005 to give a technical presentation of their PAC-2. For more, see 'Team on Missile Briefing', *Indian Express*, 17 February 2005.

[43] For an insightful discussion on India's minimum deterrence posture, see Kanti Bajpai, 'India's Nuclear Posture After Pokhran II', *International Studies*, vol. 37, no. 4, October–December 2000.

development. It is worth mentioning that in the case of nuclear weapons, mere numbers (or their yield) beyond a certain minimum are not critical to credible deterrence. China, for instance, has maintained a successful credible capability with an NFU doctrine for four decades with a figure of around 450-odd weapons to deter the two superpowers and their numerical and technological conventional military superiority. Therefore, both India and Pakistan should keep their nuclear arsenals as small as possible. This can be done if the two countries stop making more fissile material, prohibit the explosive testing of nuclear weapons, ban the development of longer-range missiles, etc. The lesser the number of weapons, the lesser is the likelihood of 'normal accidents', command and control problems, and the fewer are the targets for the terrorists.[44]

Banning Tactical Nuclear Weapons: Differentiating between a tactical and strategic nuclear weapon in the South Asian context is a difficult task because of the number of civilian casualties that would occur on both sides. Yet, for the purpose of this study, tactical nuclear weapons may be defined as 'short-range nuclear weapon systems or warheads designed for battle-field use'.[45] Both India and Pakistan should ban the production and use of these dangerous weapons. Although it is believed that India has, so far, not assembled, let alone deployed the 'baby nukes' despite the inclusion of sub-kiloton devices in the Pokhran tests, yet there are reports that the Indian Army has recently indicated its willingness in favour of such weapons to deter the adversary.[46] Such an attempt will not make nuclear weapons a tool for fighting a war,

[44] Scott D. Sagan, *The Limits of Safety: Organisations, Accidents and Nuclear Weapon*, Princeton University Press, 1993, pp. 20–45.

[45] Michael Krepon, Ziad Haider and Charles Thornton, 'Are Tactical Nuclear Weapons Needed in South Asia?', in *Escalation Control and the Nuclear Option in South Asia*, ed. Michael Krepon, Ziad Haider and Rodney W. Jones, Washington, DC: Stimson Center, 2004, pp. 1-29, at: http://www.stimson.org/southasia/pdf/ESCCONTROLCHAPTER6.pdf

[46] 'Pak Studying Cold Start Doctrine of Indian Army', *Indian Express*, 10 June 2004, p. 7.

but be a violation of India's NFU nuclear policy. Moreover, tactical nuclear weapons also require less centralized C^3 in comparison to strategic weapons, or else they will lose their operational value in the battlefield. With such unavoidably looser control and broader distribution, all the risks of inadvertent, hasty or unnecessary firing attendant with strategic weapons get multiplied with tactical weapons. So does the risk of pilferage by terrorists or other non-state actors.[47] Thus, India and Pakistan, the newest NWS, must learn from the mistakes of the West instead of repeating them.

Common Nuclear Doctrines and Strategies: The greatest scope for confidence building and risk reduction lies in harmonizing nuclear doctrines and strategies to the maximum degree possible. India and Pakistan could explore a common approach to their nuclear doctrines. This suggestion appears quite unrealistic because Pakistan rationale for its nuclear weapons is not only to deter the threat of India's nuclear weapons, but also to counter New Delhi's conventional military superiority.[48] Therefore, unless something is done by India to address Pakistani concerns on the conventional front, Islamabad is unlikely to abandon its nuclear first-use policy.

I will, here, examine the credibility of Pakistan's first-use policy and its reservations on an NFU policy. A first-strike policy requires upfront deployment of the nuclear arsenal on the highest alert with a complex and costly command and control system that Pakistan cannot afford.

Pakistan has criticised India's NFU policy as being of mere propaganda value and which is unverifiable and liable to be altered without any prior notice. It can, however, be argued that there must be something for Russia and China to conclude a bilateral NFU agreement and the US, France and UK to reject it despite

[47] R. Rajaraman, 'Ban Battlefield Nuclear Weapons', *Hindu*, 22 April 2002. Also see Gurmeet Kanwal, 'Does India Need Tactical Nuclear Weapons?', *Strategic Analysis*, vol. XXIV, no. 2, May 2000, pp. 247–64.

[48] For a discussion on India's and Pakistan's NFU policy, see Kanti Bajpai, 'No First Use in the India Pakistan Context', paper presented at the 279th Pugwash Meeting on South Asia, London, 15–17 November 2002.

continuous pressure on them to do so. Moreover, India's NFU policy is not merely a verbal or even a negotiated assurance: it can and must be seen to be reflected in the nuclear force structure, the deployment patterns, command and control systems and the state of readiness of New Delhi's nuclear forces.[49]

Pakistan may argue that an NFU policy would encourage adventurism by India. This is not the case. Even if India goes for a pre-emptive nuclear attack, there is no guarantee that it will destroy all of Pakistan's nuclear weapons and that there will be no risks of Pakistani nuclear weapons getting through and causing unacceptable damage to India. For this reason, Indian adventurism in the event of a Pakistani NFU policy is ruled out.

Pakistan has to decide whether it will stick to an outdated concept that in no way enhances the value of its deterrence, inviting many dangers to its own security. Of course, Islamabad may take a long time to come to grips with this reality and evolve a credible and affordable nuclear doctrine. Ambiguity in nuclear posture can have only limited use. Discussions on coordinating common approaches to the nuclear doctrine, on the other hand, would go a long way in reducing nuclear dangers.[50]

Non-Deployment of Nuclear Weapons: Maintaining the present posture of deterrence without active deployment of nuclear weapons is in the interest of both India and Pakistan. This can be done in two ways. In normal circumstances, warheads should be kept in a disassembled state with the explosives separated from the nuclear core. Presently, India and Pakistan are believed to be managing their nuclear weapons in this way. Following a crisis or war, if the nuclear warheads are brought to a higher state of readiness, then they should not still be mated with delivery systems. This can be done by storing nuclear weapons physically separated from nuclear capable ballistic missile and aircraft by a distance of at least 50 km. Maintaining nuclear forces in a disassembled state and keeping the warhead and the delivery systems separately and

[49] Gurmeet Kanwal, 'India's Nuclear Doctrine and Policy', *Strategic Analysis*, vol. XXIV, no. 11, February 2001, p. 1961.

[50] Singh, op. cit., n. 4 above.

under different security covers would go a long way in reducing the risk of accidents, miscalculation, and loss of control to unauthorized persons.[51]

However, how would an agreement on non-deployment, in fact how would any of the proposed Initial, Medium- and Long-Term Steps be verified? Ideally, over time, India and Pakistan would exercise much greater transparency, allow each other to inspect their nuclear facilities, formalize an agreement not to deploy nuclear weapons, etc.[52] And there is nothing in any of these measures that would adversely affect the fundamental security interests of either country. Periodically, the other country, through physical inspections, electronic signals or satellite images, could verify these measures.[53] However, the process of setting these up will certainly require considerable interaction not only between the defence and technical personnel but also between the politicians and bureaucrats, who will have to collaborate closely at all stages—in agreeing to a mutually acceptable set of measures, in installing them, and in devising ways of ensuring their verifiability.[54] But, given the present state of their relationship, it is difficult to imagine that India and Pakistan will now agree to measures

[51] For more on this aspect, see Kent L. Biringer, 'Missile Threat Reduction and Monitoring in South Asia', in *Nuclear Risk Reduction in South Asia*, ed. Michael Krepon and Michael Newbil, Washington, DC: Stimson Center, at:http://www.stimson.org/southasia/pdf/NRRMBiringer.pdf, and Nazir Kamal, 'Pakistan: Perceptions and Prospects of Reducing Nuclear Dangers in South Asia', CMC Occasional Paper at: www.cmc.sandia.gov/Links/about/papers/SAND98-0505/6/index.html

[52] Rajesh M. Basrur, 'India's Escalation-Resistant Nuclear Posture', in *Escalation Control and the Nuclear Option in South Asia*, ed. Michael Krepon, Rodney W. Jones and Ziad Haider, Washington, DC: Stimson Center, 2004, pp. 1–19, at: http://www. stimson.org/southasia/pdf/ESCCONTROLCHAPTER3.pdf

[53] For more on technical measures for verification, see Susan M. Burns, 'Arms Limitations'; Jon Neuhoff and Clifford Singer, 'The Verification and Control of Fissile Material in South Asia' Vipin Gupta, 'Sensing the Threat: Remote Monitoring Technologies'; and Akhtar Ali, 'A Framework for Nuclear Agreement and Verification' in Cohen, op. cit., n. 33 above.

[54] R. Rajaraman, 'Nuclear Weapons in South Asia: Risks and their Reduction', paper presented at the 277th Pugwash Workshop on South Asian Security, Geneva, 1–3 November 2002.

that may significantly expose their nuclear arsenal and technology to mutual inspection. Besides the strategic and technical problems, there are also serious political problems. Pakistan, for instance, may find it difficult to sign any significant agreement without concessions on Kashmir. Similarly, India may find it even difficult to give such a concession to Pakistan. Moreover, India will not negotiate any credible nuclear risk reduction with Pakistan unless China agrees to do the same with New Delhi. Therefore, what is more likely is incremental progress in CBMs between India and Pakistan on the Initial Steps. These are, in large measure, aimed at mutual reassurance and the cultivation of political ground leading to stability. Once the India–Pakistan relationship improves, progress can be expected on Medium-Term Steps or even on some Long-Term Steps. The most significant risk reduction measure at present (non-deployment of nuclear weapons) is likely to remain a tacit one between India and Pakistan. There are several reasons for this. First, India will not make a commitment that does not include China. Second, there is a strong awareness by the two countries of the risks associated with deployment of nuclear weapons. And last, the current arrangements are, in any case, working well.

Nuclear Risk Reduction between India and China

Although China is a part of the problem in South Asia, it is not easy to engage it in a nuclear dialogue with India. This is because, unlike India, China is in a different league and is a recognized NWS under the NPT. Second, the Chinese are strictly opposed to any nuclear dialogue with India. There could be several reasons for this. First, while Indians tend to the deeply apprehensive about China, the Chinese, on the contrary, tend not to perceive a serious threat from India. According to John W. Garver, there could be two objectives behind this differential Chinese perception. The first is to dissuade India from cooperating with great powers hostile to China—earlier the USSR and now the US. The second is to induce India not to object to China's military security ties with countries of South Asia—Pakistan, Myanmar, Nepal, and Bangladesh. These relations, according to the Chinese, do not in any way constitute a threat to India, and it is thus unreasonable for New Delhi to object to them.[55]

Second, China refuses to acknowledge India as a de facto NWS and still insists that India immediately stop its nuclear weapons programme, abide by the UN Security Council resolution of 6 June 1998,[56] and sign the NPT and the CTBT unconditionally and immediately. Hence, a nuclear dialogue with India would be tantamount to acknowledging its nuclear weapon status. Last, China always projects itself as a responsible NWS whose nuclear weapons exist only to deter prospective threats from (other recognized) NWS. For this reason, its nuclear arsenal is not deemed to pose a risk similar to that held out by the newly nuclearized states such as India and Pakistan. If there are no risks, why negotiate?

Thus, India's perception of China as a potential adversary and China's opposition to its inclusion in a nuclear dialogue with India makes the task of cooperative risk reduction between the two countries difficult. Different suggestions are given in this context. The first is that in order to make China agree to a nuclear dialogue with India, New Delhi should develop its nuclear capabilities to the extent that Beijing must take note of its capabilities. To achieve this, India has to develop a missile capability either matching or superior to that of China's existing arsenal.[57] A

[55] John W. Garver, 'Asymmetrical Indian and Chinese Threat Perceptions', *Indian Review*, vol. 1, no. 4, October 2002, pp. 131–2.

[56] The UN Security Council Resolution No. 1172 of 6 June 1998 required India and Pakistan to 'conduct no further nuclear tests; sign and ratify the Comprehensive Test Ban Treaty deploying nuclear weapons or missile systems; halt the production of fissile material for nuclear weapons; participate constructively in negotiations towards a fissile material cut-off treaty; formalize existing policies not to export weapons of mass destruction and missile technology or equipment; and resume a direct dialogue to address the root causes of tension between them, including Kashmir'. For more on the text of UN Resolution 1172 of 6 June 1998, see 'After the Tests: US Policy Towards India and Pakistan', *A Report of the Independent Task Force*, co-sponsored by the Brookings Institution, Washington, DC and Council on Foreign Relations, New York, 1998, pp. 57–60.

[57] M.V. Rappai, 'Nuclear Factor in India–China Relations', in *Asian Strategic Review*, ed. Jasjit Singh, New Delhi: IDSA, 1998–9, p. 325.

second suggestion is that while India may well face a significant security threat from China, that relationship lacks the immediacy of the India–Pakistani nuclear dyad. Therefore, India should wait for some more time to engage China, but negotiate risk reduction measures with Pakistan. A set of bilateral measures reached with Islamabad may enable New Delhi to then start a similar process with Beijing at a future date.[58] A third suggestion is to convince China that a nuclear risk reduction dialogue with India would serve its interests better.[59] For instance, the Chinese could be persuaded that it is not in their long-term interests to see the deployment of nuclear weapons in South Asia. Similarly, they could be made to realize that a nuclear conflict between India and Pakistan would also impact China's border regions. Finally, China would be equally concerned about the spread of nuclear weapons to states or groups of terrorists which do not abide by the traditional rules of nuclear deterrence.

While there is some merit in these suggestions, a more realistic proposal could be to highlight common points between the two countries on all issues (including the nuclear one) and improve their bilateral relationship across a broad front.

It is pertinent to mention that Sino–Indian relations have come a long way since the 1962 war and the prolonged tensions that followed in its wake. Despite the chill caused by India's nuclear tests in 1998, trade between the two countries grew from $1.1 billion in 1995 to $13 billion in 2004.[60] Similarly, India's 3,400-km. long land border with China has largely remained peaceful over the last 25 years.[61] Sino–Indian security ties have also undergone a change, with the resumption of military ties signified by

[58] Sumit Ganguly and Kent Biringer, 'Nuclear Crisis Stability in South Asia', *Asian Survey*, November–December 2001, pp. 907–24.

[59] Lewis A. Dunn, 'The Widening Nuclear Circle: South Asian Choices in Broader Perspective', in *Bridging the Non-Proliferation Divide*, ed. Francine Frankel, New Delhi: Konark Publishers, 1995, pp. 89–137.

[60] 'Towards a Strong Partnership', *Hindu* (editorial), 27 January 2005.

[61] Natwar Singh's address to the Seventh Asian Security Conference, IDSA, New Delhi, 28 January 2005, quoted in 'India–China Ties Do Not Hamper Ties', *Hindu*, 29 January 2005.

joint exercises, bilateral visits, and sharing of information on military matters of joint interests.[62] By institutionalizing the Sino–Indian dialogue at a political level with regular exchanges between designated interlocutors, the territorial question can also get discussed.

It can also be mentioned that India and China are two nuclear powers with many common interests in a host of international issues, including nuclear weapons. Both nations have practically a common nuclear doctrine of NFU, maintain their nuclear capabilities at relatively low levels of readiness, are against any kind of nuclear blackmail in the international arena, and agree on the 'total elimination of nuclear weapons' as their ultimate goal.[63] Once common issues bring the two countries together and political problem solving and deepening economic co-operation begin to take root, India and China could start a nuclear dialogue and negotiate various risk reduction measures as discussed in the context of India and Pakistan. As initial steps, the security dialogue that the two sides have recently started for clarifying each other's positions on issues of mutual concern and dispelling any misunderstanding that might lead to potential conflicts should be extended to exchanging views on security concepts and nuclear doctrines, increasing information exchange in the nuclear field leading to greater transparency, and acting as a consultative machinery to review and implement nuclear CBMs. Similarly, they could use their current official bilateral channels such as the Joint Working Group (JWG) that has been established for demarcation of the Line of Actual Control for discussing concerns about each other's weapons development and deployment.[64] These measures do not compromise their national security

[62] Pranab Mukherjee's address to ibid., 29 January 2005, quoted in 'More Areas of Agreement than Differences with China', *Hindu*, 30 January 2005.

[63] For more, see Ashley Tellis, *India's Emerging Nuclear Doctrine: Exemplifying the Lessons of the Nuclear Revolution*, National Bureau of Asian Research, vol. 12, no. 2, May 2001, p. xi; and Rappai, op. cit., n. 57 above.

[64] For more, see Jing-dong Yuan, 'India's Rise After Pokhran II', *Asian Survey*, vol. XLI, no. 6, November–December 2001, pp. 978–1001.

in any sense. On the contrary, they could build confidence and trust between the two countries for negotiating significant NRRMs at a later stage.

Role of the US

The US could play an important role in the context of nuclear risk reduction between India, Pakistan and China. It can press Pakistan to dismantle the infrastructure of terrorism that it has used against India, encourage both New Delhi and Islamabad to accept a fair and reasonable solution to the Kashmir dispute, engage China to enter into a nuclear dialogue with India, and, more importantly, assist both India and Pakistan in ensuring better security and control of their nuclear weapons and materials. However, there are some apprehensions that US nuclear assistance to India and Pakistan will violate its NPT obligations, be inconsistent with the existing domestic and international export control, amount to 'rewarding' proliferators and thus lead to more proliferation or fall into the wrong hands, among other thing. Let me examine these apprehensions one by one. The objection that US assistance would violate the NPT actually misinterprets the treaty. Article 1 of the NPT obliges its signatories not to 'transfer to any recipient whatsoever nuclear weapons or other nuclear explosive devices or control over such weapons or explosive devices directly or indirectly'. This cannot be interpreted to proscribe anything, which contributes to its own stress on the dangers of nuclear war to 'all mankind' and the 'need to make every effort to avert the danger of such a war'.[65] The term 'control' within the meaning of the treaty clearly refers to enabling functions, not restrictive ones designed to prevent war.[66] On the apprehension that US nuclear assistance would be in violation of American export control laws, it can be mentioned that the Bush Administration is currently revising the export control laws and arguing that most forms of nuclear security assistance do not violate the

[65] For a look at the NPT, see: http://fas.org/nuke/control/npt/text/npt2.htm
[66] Basrur, op. cit., n. 17 above, p. 10.

NPT.[67] The argument that a state's decision to proliferate is affected by the prospect of reward is unfounded. As discussed in Chapter 1, India and Pakistan decided to go 'nuclear' not because of any prospective reward but for security reasons. Moreover, state leaders do not take nuclear decisions so lightly. It is the gravity of the choice to 'go nuclear' that best explains why so few of such decisions have been made.[68] Finally past examples show that policies that are too tightly bound to a goal of 'non-proliferation' are doomed to failure. The fact that China, despite its non-proliferation commitments, continues to assist Pakistan and several other countries also weighs heavily against any non-proliferation goals. Therefore, it is my contention that between non-proliferation and the goal of improving nuclear safety and stability, the former should be adjusted in favour of the latter.

There is some truth at least in the case of Pakistan that information about nuclear security and control procedures could be compromised. It can, however, be argued that the very purpose of some of the types of assistance that could be provided, for example on personnel reliability programmes, would help to weed out such threats. Besides, this threat may already exist and would not be made worse, but could be reduced by some type of assistance.[69] The US should also realize that neither New Delhi nor Islamabad threatens Washington's vital security interests or those of its allies and a nuclear accident or a nuclear terrorist incident is a danger to all states, including America. As Gregory Giles correctly writes, 'For all the risks raised by assistance on nuclear weapons' safety and security, the dangers of inaction by the international com-

[67] Scott D. Sagan, 'Terrorism, Pakistan and Nuclear Weapons', in *After 9/11: Preventing Mass Destruction Terrorism and Weapons Proliferation*, ed. Michael Barletta, CNS Occasional Paper no. 8, Monterey, May 2002, pp. 46, 50.

[68] Jacques Hymans, 'Why Do States Acquire Nuclear Weapons?', in *Nuclear India in the Twenty-First Century*, ed. D. R. Sardesai and Raju Thomas, New York: Palgrave, 2002, p. 153.

[69] Lewis A. Dunn, 'Balancing Nuclear Security and Non-Proliferation in South Asia', in *A New Equation: US Policy Towards India and Pakistan After September 11*, ed. Lee Feinstein, Carnegie Endowment for International Peace Working Paper no. 27, May 2002, pp. 23–32.

munity are even greater. Where rollback is a less realistic expectation, safety and security assistance should take a more active role.'[70] Therefore, there is a strong need for US policy makers to liberally interpret legal documents like the NPT and provide the following nuclear assistance to India and Pakistan.[71]

1. Help India and Pakistan to improve organizational best practices to ensure better coordination among various organs dealing with diverse aspects of their nuclear programmes.
2. Extend useful assistance for safe and secure storage, transport and disposal of nuclear waste.
3. Provide modern technologies to India and Pakistan such as sensors, alarms, tamper-proof seals, closed circuit cameras and labels for safe and secure storage, transport and maintenance of nuclear components and warheads.
4. Consider sharing its experience and procedures relating to personnel reliability programmes.
5. Share aspects of the experience of its NEST which could help India and Pakistan cope with a variety of nuclear incidents.
6. Train Indian and Pakistani customs officials in detecting WMDs to check its transnational smuggling and proliferation.[72]

Presently, neither India nor Pakistan use PALs nor do they have the technological capability to have this anytime soon. Therefore, the US should provide PALs to both countries to enhance their nuclear safety and security. Some people argue that possession of PALs will encourage active deployment by India and Pakistan and increase the element of risk.[73] This is not actually the case.

[70] Gregory F. Gills, 'Safeguarding the Undeclared Nuclear Arsenals', *Washington Quarterly*, Spring 1993, pp. 183–4.

[71] For a comprehensive list of recommendations, see Dunn, op. cit., n. 69 above; and Sagan, op. cit., n. 67 above.

[72] In early 2004, the US Immigration and Customs Enforcement Directorate held workshops at Delhi, Mumbai and Chennai for about 20 customs officers of joint commissioner rank and above where the two sides exchanged intelligence on transboundary movement of WMDs. For more, see 'US to Train our Customs Staff to Spot WMDs', *Indian Express*, 21 July 2004.

[73] See, for instance, Lee Feinstein, 'When Policy Priorities Converge: US Relations

Both India and Pakistan are strongly aware of the risks that go with nuclear deployment. This is the reason why even at the height of their confrontation in 1999 and 2001–2, both India and Pakistan had exercised great restraint in not deploying their nuclear weapons. Moreover, in volatile situations involving armed confrontation amid high levels of terrorist activity, the benefits of more effective command and control should take precedence over the risks of false confidence derived from technical sophistication.[74] If there is still some uneasiness, the US could at least pass along earlier versions of its PALs and other weapons security design.[75] Just as the US will face constraints in offering security assistance, similarly India and Pakistan are likely to be reluctant in accepting the US assistance as this could violate the confidentiality of their nuclear programmes. But despite some reservations on both the sides, there is ample scope for the US, India and Pakistan to work together for making Indo–Pakistani nuclear weapons safer (less prone to accidental detonation) and more secure (impervious to unauthorized use).[76] There are reports that the US has been formally engaging Pakistan on this issue.[77] There is no reason why it could not engage India. After all, both the states have signed a strategic partnership agreement with each other in January 2004 to co-operate in civilian nuclear development, space programmes, high technology trade and missile defence.

International organizations such as the International Atomic Energy Agency (IAEA) can play a major role in upgrading the

---

With India and Pakistan', in his ed. *A New Equation: US Policy Towards India and Pakistan After September 11*, Carnegie Endowment for International Peace Working Paper no. 27, May 2002, pp. 23–32.

[74] Basrur, op. cit., n. 17 above.

[75] Robert E. Rehbein, 'Managing Proliferation in South Asia: A Case for Assistance to Unsafe Nuclear Arsenals', *Non-Proliferation Review*, vol. 9, no. 1, Spring 2002, p. 101.

[76] For more, see Rose Gottemoeller and Rebecca Longsworth, 'Enhancing Nuclear Securing in the Counter-Terrorism Struggle: India and Pakistan as a New Region for Co-operation', CEIP Working Paper no. 29, August 2002, at: www.ceip.org/files/publications/ws29.asp?from=update

[77] Rehbein, op. cit., n. 75 above.

existing safety and security arrangements of Indo–Pakistani nuclear facilities and materials. They can train and provide assistance in the design and implementation of security systems around nuclear facilities. Funding for such activities could come from a variety of sources, but should also be a national investment priority for each country.[78]

The above measures are neither exhaustive nor do they constitute a technological panacea for resolving the nuclear conundrum in South Asia. In fact, the conditions of instability in South Asia have to do more with the software (the attitude and policy choices) than the hardware (lack of technological sophistication). Therefore, the best insurance policy to reduce nuclear risks in the subcontinent is to improve the bilateral relationships between India and Pakistan, and India and China. The better the relations, the more likely that nuclear weapons will recede as an important factor in their relationship, and the easier it will be to take significant steps to reduce nuclear risks.

[78] Arian L. Pregenzer, 'Securing Nuclear Capabilities in India and Pakistan: Reducing the Terrorist and Proliferation Risks', *Non-Proliferation Review*, vol. 10, no. 1, Spring 2003, pp. 124–31.

CHAPTER 4

Problems and Prospects

Three major problems stand in the way of reducing nuclear risks in South Asia. They are: the unresolved nature of the Jammu & Kashmir dispute; the glorification of nuclear weapons by India and Pakistan; and an unfavourable global strategic environment.

The Problem of Kashmir

The unresolved nature of the Kashmir dispute creates hurdles in the way of negotiating NRRMs between India and Pakistan. The Kingdom of Kashmir had been divided into two main parts in 1949. The portion of Kashmir to the west and to the north of the LOC is under Pakistan's control, what India calls POK. Pakistan has transferred 5,180 sq. km. of POK to China under an agreement in 1963. To the south of the LOC stretches the land under India's control, which constitutes Jammu & Kashmir. The whole of Kashmir has become an issue of profound disagreement between the two countries. Pakistan's claim on Kashmir (under India's control) the only Muslim-majority state in the Indian Union is based on religion and geographical contiguity. Hence, it considers Kashmir the 'unfinished agenda of Partition'. India's claim on Kashmir (the portion that is now under its control as it has almost given up its claim on the Pakistani and Chinese portions of Kashmir) is based upon the defence of its status as a secular state with a Muslim population larger than that of Pakistan. Besides, its claim is also reinforced by the accession of the whole of Kashmir to India by the Maharaja of Kashmir in 1947 as 'final and irrevocable'.[1]

[1] New Delhi's old argument has been that POK is an integral part of India since it was deemed so by a 1994 Parliamentary resolution, and that any government of the day has to be 'answerable to its elected representatives'. Pakistan's position on

The unresolved nature of the Kashmir dispute has affected and is still affecting the nuclear risk reduction dialogue in two ways. First, the resolution of the Kashmir issue is being made a condition by Pakistan for moving forward on the nuclear issue.[2] This Pakistani perception is also associated with the belief that Pakistan's acquisition of nuclear weapons had much to do with Jammu & Kashmir and that South Asia would remain a nuclear flashpoint unless and until the Kashmir issue is resolved to Pakistan's satisfaction.[3] India sees this as an attempt at leveraging nuclear weapons to compel a political settlement on Kashmir.

India, on the other hand, has regarded that the nuclear risk reduction dialogue should be confined to nuclear weapon-specific issues and be examined outside the ambit of other issues. As far as Kashmir is concerned, India is of the view that the salience of contentious issues will be reduced, and, the situation more amenable to a solution once relations between the two countries develop through various spheres.[4]

This divergence of views has made the progress of the dialogue on nuclear risk reduction a much more complex endeavour. To quote Lieutenant General V.R. Raghavan:

> Nuclear deterrent and risks inherent in them have a merit and logic of their own. If a solution is to be had, it can only be through sharing the understanding and logic of nuclear weapons risks. Adding conditionality to reducing nuclear risks can therefore only enhance such risks with unpredictable and catastrophic consequences.[5]

---

this issue has been that the 1949 UN resolutions calling for a plebiscite must be invoked, so that the people of Kashmir-by which it means that Kashmir Valley—are allowed to choose whether they want to go India or Pakistan. Only then, Islamabad firmly believes, will the logic of Partition be complete.

[2] 'Success of CBMs Depends on Kashmir, Says Musharraf', *Hindu*, 28 April 2004.

[3] For more on this, see Michael Krepon, 'Nuclear Risk Reduction', *Kashmir Sentinel*, 30 September 2001; and Jean-Luc Racine, 'Pakistan and the Indian Syndrome: Between Kashmir and the Nuclear Predicament', in *Pakistan: Nationalism Without a Nation?*, ed. Christophe Jaffrelot, New Delhi: Manohar, 2002, pp. 195–227.

[4] 'Peace by Piece', *Indian Express* (editorial), 29 June 2004.

[5] V.R. Raghavan, 'Nuclear Dialogue With Pakistan', *Hindu*, 25 January 2001.

However, in recent months, there has been a perceptible change in the position of the two countries. Even if Pakistan is not inclined to delink negotiations on Kashmir from other issues on the agenda of the bilateral dialogue, Islamabad does appear to have set aside its policy of blocking forward movement in other spheres until it sees progress on talks relating to Kashmir. Similarly, India, which had been refusing to talk to Pakistan on Kashmir, has taken the big step of putting Kashmir on the negotiating table.[6]

But this does not mean that everything is going well between India and Pakistan. For instance, Pakistan has recently stressed on 'simultaneous' progress on all issues, especially Jammu & Kashmir and the need for its final settlement within a 'reasonable time frame'. India had perceived this Pakistani strategy as 'unfair pressure tactics' tanta-mount to imposing 'preconditions' on the ongoing composite dialogue and reacted by countering allegations of 'cross-border terrorism' once again.[7] These conditions and pre-conditions may prove catastrophic for the peace process. If the peace process is disrupted, Pakistan may again resume using its covert military options and this may force India to develop the necessary military options to deal with renewed terrorism from Pakistan. All these may not only delay NRRMs but could also raise all types of nuclear risks discussed earlier.

Pakistan needs to bear in mind that the issue that has divided the two nations for nearly six decades cannot be sorted out within a few months. India should realize that the process of peace with Pakistan will benefit it in the long term. Therefore, there is a strong need for a structured, sustained, and meaningful dialogue between the two countries that could lead to a durable solution of the Kashmir dispute.[8]

[6] 'Build on the Rapport', *Hindu* (editorial), 24 June 2004.

[7] Najam Sethi, 'Pakistan Between East and West', *Indian Express*, 28 August 2004.

[8] However, there are some analysts who think that Kashmir is not a problem for nuclear risk reduction in South Asia. They see the Pakistan Army as the real obstacle, because it has a number of incentives for or vested interests in continuing its anti-India policy, and Pakistan's nuclear weapons programme is the preserve of this rabid anti-India military establishment. See, for instance, T.S. Gopi Rethinaraj,

Various suggestions have been given to solve the Kashmir dispute. These include: converting the LOC into an international border; alteration of the LOC in Pakistan's favour; dividing Kashmir Valley by making river Chenab the boundary; softening the current border with maximum autonomy, etc.[9] It is not the purpose of this paper to go into the merits and demerits of each suggestion. Suffice it to say that this is not the time to take a position on the shape of the final settlement of the dispute. Let such a settlement emerge after dialogue among the parties including Kashmiris on both sides of the LOC. Moreover, we should remember that both sides have extremely limited negotiating space to move towards a solution on Kashmir. Common sense would tell us that any negotiating space would require substantive mutual trust and the reshaping of bilateral relations across the board. This could be done by going beyond dispute settlement to creating interdependence and would need to be future-oriented rather than being bogged down in the past. Only such an approach can eradicate mistrust over time, making relations less vulnerable to emotional reactions and domestic politics.[10]

'Threats and Perceptions of Nuclear War in South Asia', *Swords and Ploughshares*, vol. XIV, no. 1, Summer 2002, pp. 22–5; C. Raja Mohan, 'Indo-Pak Talks and Rawalpindi', *Hindu*, 5 June 2003; and Gautam Sen, 'Military Action Pakistan', *Hindu*, 28 December 2001.

[9] See, for instance, Verghese Koithara, 'Peace is a Realist's Brew', *Indian Express*, 4 August 2004; J.N. Dixit, 'The Line of Return', *Indian Express*, 3 October 2002; K.K. Katyal, 'LOC and its Conversion as Border', *Hindu*, 20 January 2003; and Muzamil Jaleel, 'The Chenab Compromise for Kashmir', *Indian Express*, 28 Junuary 2003.

However, most observers are of the view that India could, at most, transform the LOC into a 'softer kind of line' which 'bridges, instead divides' the people of Kashmir. But given the strategic investments Islamabad has made in Kashmir over the last two decades, such a step is unlikely to solve the Kashmir problem. In fact, many believe that Pakistani is not going to dismantle the infrastructure of terrorism until the Kashmir issue is on an irrevocable path to resolution since the jihad is the most potent card in Pakistan's arsenal of negotiating tools with Kashmir. For more, see C. Raja Mohan, 'Sustaining the Peace Process', *Hindu*, 30 August 2004; Sethi, op. cit., n. 7 above.

[10] 'Peace by Piece', op. cit., n. 4 above.

Unilateral steps and mutual CBMs could be important in this regard. Pakistan should sustain the current ceasefire, continue to refrain from providing military and intelligence support for infiltration, and withdraw the militants already inside Kashmir. India, on its part, could also undertake measures like a unilateral ceasefire against the militants in Kashmir, reduction in the level of troop deployment, release of a large number of political prisoners in Jammu & Kashmir, and withdraw some of the draconian laws operating in the state. Equally important are other CBMs that will allow the creation of linkages between the people and institutions across the divide in Jammu & Kashmir. Pakistan should promote greater people-to-people contacts in the divided state. Similarly, India could act on issues such as liberalization of visas, promotion of group tourism from Pakistan, and opening Indian educational institutions to Pakistani students.[11] It is pertinent to mention here that over the last few months, India has been unilaterally relaxing rules for several categories of visitors from Pakistan, including journalists, professionals, and members of civil society groups. Recently, it allowed Pakistani journalists to visit Kashmir and evaluate the situation there for themselves. The Indian Govern-ment's latest gesture of visa-on-arrival for Pakistani nationals under 12 years or over 65 years of age is especially commendable. So is the offer of visas to those wishing to study in India.[12] Similarly, during the visit of Natwar Singh to Islamabad, India and Pakistan decided to start a bus service between Srinagar and Muzaffarabad, reopen consulates in Karachi and Mumbai, launch a new bus service between Lahore and Amritsar, and re-establish rail-links between Rajasthan and Sind.[13]

On the economic front, both India and Pakistan could become a single economic unit (with Bangladesh included) so that the ties of trade and commerce develop into ties of dependence and friendship.[14] Once there is greater movement towards normal

[11] C. Raja Mohan, 'Towards CBMs on Kashmir', *Hindu*, 24 June 2004.

[12] 'Remaining Engaged', *Hindu* (editorial), 1 January 2005.

[13] 'A Route to Peace', *Hindu* (editorial), 18 February 2005.

[14] Kuldip Nayar, 'Kashmir Can Not be Solved this Way', *Indian Express*, 27 July 2004.

relations based on cooperation and dependence, there will be greater scope for arriving at mutually agreed solutions to outstanding issues and disputes, including that of Jammu & Kashmir.

Glorification of Nuclear Weapons

The Indian and Pakistani 'false claims' about their nuclear weapons is another problem. Subsequent to the Pokhran and Chagai explosions of mid-1998, there has been a concerted effort by India and Pakistan to legitimize—even glorify—their nuclear weapons as acceptable means of achieving regional and global power.[15] The official Indian nuclear dogma, for instance, has always maintained that India's nuclear weapons are 'good nukes', the welcome fruit of decades of self-reliant labour by Indian scientists and engineers, and a symbol of India's scientific and technological strength. Nuclear weaponization is presented as a necessity for the protection of the geopolitical interests of a great nation that has finally found the will to become a world-class power. The Pakistan Government has also been indulging in similar propaganda. According to Tariq Rehman, a Pakistani commentator, 'It (nuclear weapon) has become the central icon of the nation, the symbol of our identity, the fount of our deepest emotions. It almost took upon a religious significance.'[16]

It is not just that nuclear weapons are glorified, the persons associated with the programmes have almost become cult figures. This is as true of A.Q. Khan of Pakistan as it is of A.P.J. Abdul Kalam of India. They have not only been decorated with the highest national awards of their respective countries, but became 'the idol of the people, the dearest of their heroes, and the greatest of their redeemers'.[17]

[15] For more on this aspect, see W. P. S. Sidhu, 'India's Security and Nuclear Risk Reduction Measures', in *Nuclear Risk Reduction in South Asia*, ed. Michael Krepon and Michael Newbil, Washington, DC: Stimson Center, November 1998, pp. 6–9, at: http://www.stimson.org/pubs/cbm/sa/sidhufnl.pdf

[16] Tariq Rehman quoted in Sevanti Ninan, 'Pakistan in Fission', *Hindu*, 15 February 2004.

[17] A.Q. Khan, whom many Pakistanis believe provided a nuclear shield to Pakistan

Thus, the glorification of nuclear weapons and the cult figure status of the individuals associated with them have created such a situation in both countries that their people are not adequately aware of what dangers nuclear programmes may have or the risks in producing, stockpiling, inducting and developing these WMD.[18] Nuclear risk reduction in such an environment becomes a difficult endeavour. The people of both India and Pakistan must be made fully aware of the risks that go with possessing nuclear weapons. They should know that besides the devastation they cause when deliberately exploded, nuclear weapons as physical objects are intrinsically dangerous even when 'at rest'.[19]

Unfavourable Global Strategic Environment

An unfavourable global environment acts as a barrier for reducing nuclear risks in South Asia. The attacks of 11 September 2001 show how a single incident can transform the behaviour and perceptions of many states. A nuclear incident in South Asia could influence the world's perceptions of both the region and the dangers of its nuclear weapons. Similarly, a nuclear incident elsewhere in the world might cause India and Pakistan to rethink their nuclear plans.

The global strategic environment has been made unfavourable by several recent developments. The US, for instance, has not ratified the CTBT and has made it clear that it reserves the right to resume nuclear testing whenever it thinks this might be necessary in the future. Washington has announced plans to develop and test mini-nuclear weapons. It has discarded the Anti-

---

and protected it from the 'evil eye of India', is the only one in Pakistan who has been decorated with the highest civilian awards of the country twice: B. Muralidhar Reddy, 'Hero Turned Victim', *Frontline*, vol. 21, no. 4, 27 February 2004, p. 47; also see M.V. Ramana, 'Missiles and Fast Delivery of Nuclear Destruction', *Daily Times*, 23 May 2002.

[18] 'Reduce Nuclear Risk With Pakistan', *Hindu* (editorial), 19 June 2004.

[19] R. Rajaraman, 'Nuclear Weapons in South Asia: Risks and their Reduction', paper presented at the 277th Pugwash Workshop on South Asian Security, Geneva, 1–3 November 2002.

Ballistic Missile (ABM) Treaty and makes no secret of its determination to build a strategic overarching Ballistic Missile Defence (BMD) for itself. It also aims to set up various Theatre Missile Defence (TMD) systems with its allies. According to Satish Chandra, a former Deputy to the National Security Adviser, Government of India, 'the development of the missile defence is part of the paradigm shift (in the US) whereby it could consider resorting to the use of nuclear weapons in a pre-emptive mode'. Many also question the legality of its Proliferation Security Initiative (PSI), the controversial programme under which the US and its fifteen allies have given themselves the right to interdict, on the high seas, ships suspected of carrying illicit weapons. The PSI is not only contrary to the principle of 'Freedom of the Seas', but its operational efficacy is also doubtful because of its escalatory potential. The US is also exploring non-traditional measures to deal with the threat of WMD in the hands of the so-called 'rogue states' or terrorist organizations.[20] These US decisions are likely to influence the perceptions of other countries of the military utility of nuclear weapons and damage international and regional efforts toward non-proliferation and disarmament.

Russia, which supported the abolition of nuclear weapons from the mid-1980s to the early 1990s, has by now perceptibly cooled in its ardour. Given the steady erosion of its conventional military capability in the 1990s, Moscow's reliance on nuclear weapons has already increased.[21] Moreover, Russia's threat to develop a new offensive weapon to neutralize the contemplated BMD system of the US seems to have come very close to realization with the recent successful testing of what is being described as a hypersonic cruise missile.

Britain and France, despite the absence of any threats to their security, have been reluctant to the abolition of nuclear weapons. Moreover, they have been unwilling to adopt an NFU pledge

[20] For more, see C. Uday Bhaskar, 'Bush Outlines New US Nuclear Policy', *Strategic Analysis*, vol. XXV, no. 3, June 2001, pp. 331–42.

[21] C. Raja Mohan, 'No First Use and India's Nuclear Transition', paper presented at the 279th Pugwash Meeting on South Asia, London, 15–17 November 2002.

and have refused to forgo their right to use nuclear weapons against non-NWS. According to press reports, the UK Government has even laid out two billion pounds to equip the Atomic Weapons Establishment with the means to design and build a new 'generation of tactical nuclear weapons'.[22]

The Chinese are not far behind. From their past commitments to nuclear disarmament and NFU, they are moving towards an expansion of their nuclear arsenal as well as towards ideas of a 'limited war under high-tech conditions' that includes a nuclear war-fighting strategy.[23]

What is more deplorable is that all this is happening at a time when the major powers no longer face a nuclear threat to their security from one another. The threat they perceive from the so-called rogue states is highly exaggerated. Besides, the threat can be more than adequately taken care of by the highly sophisticated conventional weapons of the major powers.[24]

An unfavourable global strategic environment affects nuclear risk reduction in South Asia in more than one way. First, in a strategic environment where everyone is feverishly augmenting and upgrading its nuclear arsenal, it is unrealistic to expect India and Pakistan to apply self-imposed restrictions that may put them under permanent nuclear disadvantage. Second, the US decision to scrap the ABM Treaty and accelerate efforts to build a missile shield has added to fears in China that its nuclear deterrent might be less credible in future. Any Chinese retaliation against the US missile defence—deploying more ICBMs, many or with multiple warheads—may not directly threaten India, but the overall threat environment would encourage India to move towards a more robust nuclear posture, particularly if India–China relations are vitiated by continuing Chinese nuclear and missile assistance to Pakistan. The Chinese perception that India is part of a US strategy to contain China would raise Sino–Indian tensions several notches. A more aggressive and unstable nuclear relationship may emerge

[22] George Monbiot, 'The Paradox of Modern Warfare', *Hindu*, 31 March 2004.

[23] For more, see Swaran Singh, 'Chinese Doctrine of Limited High Tech War', in *Asian Strategic Review 1998–99*, ed. Jasjit Singh, New Delhi: IDSA, pp. 333–50.

[24] Muchkund Dubey, 'For Nuclear Disarmament', *Hindu*, 6 March 2004.

as a result. A strong Indian nuclear response to change in its relationship with China would inevitably raise the strategic temperature between India and Pakistan.[25]

A more favourable strategic environment, on the other hand, could strengthen and accelerate nuclear risk reduction in South Asia. For instance, an enforceable global taboo against the threat or first-use of nuclear weapons could reinforce similar constraints on the use of nuclear weapons in South Asia. Likewise, any multilateral, non-discriminatory agreement banning production of plutonium and highly enriched uranium for nuclear weapons and a ban on nuclear testing could encourage both India and Pakistan to adhere to new global limits on nuclear materials production and testing.[26] Similarly, steps to improve the safety and security of nuclear materials worldwide, strengthening export controls among NWS to prevent proliferation, enhancing inspection procedures by the IAEA, stiffening penalties for persons accused of nuclear terrorism, and beefing up law enforcement and intelligence sharing would not only remove the threat of nuclear terrorism but also reduce the risk of unauthorized use of nuclear weapons by terrorists at the global level, including the most potential region, i.e. South Asia.[27]

It is for the established NWS to decide if the game is worth it. As George Monbiot correctly remarks, 'The paradox is that by enhancing our military strength, we enhanced our opponent's capacity (read non-state actors) to destroy us. The US has been producing weaponized anthrax ostensibly to anticipate terrorist threats. In 2001, anthrax stolen from this programme was used to terrorise America.'[28]

[25] For more, see Upendra Choudhury, 'Theatre Missile Defence: Implications for South Asian Security', *Journal of Peace Studies*, vol. 9, no. 4, July–August 2002, pp. 15–19.

[26] Lewis A. Dunn, 'The Widening Nuclear Circle: South Asian Choices in Broader Perspective', in *Bridging the Non-Proliferation Divide*, ed. Francine Frankel, New Delhi: Konark Publishers, 1995, pp. 89–137.

[27] For more, see IAEA Release 'Calculating the New Global Nuclear Terrorism Threat, *Strategic Digest*, vol. XXXI, no. 11, November 2001.

[28] Monbiot, op. cit., n. 22 above.

CHAPTER 5

Key Findings and Future Possibilities

- The nuclear rivalry in South Asia consists of two dyads: India versus Pakistan; and India versus China. With both rival nuclear powers, India must contend with territorial disputes, a history of war, and periodic crises and perceptions of nuclear threat.
- However, the bilateral India–China deterrent relationship is more stable than the India–Pakistan nuclear relationship. This is because both India and China have perhaps reached an understanding that their persistent differences should not be allowed to prevent the stabilization of their strategic relationship as a whole. However, India and Pakistan still continue to harbour rigid attitudes on Kashmir and adopt dangerous tactics to check each other.
- These include Pakistan's cross-border terrorism policy against India and India's limited war doctrine to punish Pakistan. Both these strategies are escalatory and perhaps could lead to a 'war' or 'warlike situation' in South Asia.
- Any war or hot crisis between India and Pakistan might contribute to the risks of intentional, accidental, or unauthorized use of nuclear weapons. Moreover, there are risks associated with the incremental expansion of India's and Pakistan's nuclear programmes.
- Although the India–China nuclear relationship is relatively stable, India perceives long-term security threats from that country. If the Sino–Indian relationship takes a downward turn resulting in a limited border war or a nuclear crisis, all the three nuclear risks mentioned in the Indo–Pakistani crisis situation could raise their ugly heads.
- The above-mentioned nuclear dangers should have made

India, China and Pakistan negotiate risk reduction measures with each other. But the Chinese are unwilling to enter into a nuclear dialogue with India and even refuse to acknowledge it as a de facto NWS. It is because of this that trilateral nuclear risk reduction is a difficult task in South Asia. Therefore, under the present circumstances, India should negotiate bilateral risk reduction measures with Pakistan. Once their bilateral relationship improves across a broad front, both India and China could then start a nuclear dialogue and negotiate NRRMs either bilaterally or trilaterally.

- Nuclear risks between India and Pakistan cannot be addressed by nuclear-specific measures alone. While nuclear measures are useful in their own way, it is even more important to consider mechanisms that reduce the prospects for conventional military tensions between the two countries.
- Military tensions between India and Pakistan could be reduced by dismantling the infrastructure of terrorism by Pakistan, abandoning the limited war doctrine by India, rigorously implementing the existing conventional CBMs while pursuing new ones, and finding a just and permanent solution of the Kashmir dispute.
- Resolution of the Kashmir issue is, of course, desirable, but should not be made a condition for reducing nuclear dangers. This is because the nuclear risk reduction issue is not just the most important issue between India and Pakistan, but one which deserves the most urgent attention.
- Nuclear risks could be reduced both by unilateral and bilateral measures. Some bilateral risk reduction measures that do not require any major change in the nuclear strategy and posture between India and Pakistan could be negotiated immediately as initial steps. If these are successful they could build necessary confidence and trust between the two countries. Thereafter, more extensive steps in the medium and long terms could be undertaken to reduce nuclear risks in South Asia.
- Three major problems stand in the way of reducing nuclear risks in South Asia. They include: the unresolved nature of the Kashmir dispute; the glorification of nuclear weapons by both

India and Pakistan; and an unfavourable global strategic environment.

- India and Pakistan should remember that there is no magical or miraculous way of overcoming hostilities: they have to find a solution to the Kashmir issue through a long and continuous process of dialogue. But given the complex nature of the dispute that has divided the two states for nearly six decades, both New Delhi and Islamabad should continue their dialogue on Kashmir and simultaneously improve their bilateral relationship across a broad front. Once there is greater movement towards normal relations, there will be greater scope for arriving at mutually agreed upon solutions to outstanding issues and disputes, including Kashmir.
- Perhaps both have realized this. The ceasefire between India and Pakistan along the international border and the LOC, their frequent meetings at the top political level, and the composite dialogue process now underway between the two countries covering eight issues (J&K, Siachen, Wular Barrage/Tulbul Navigation Project, Sir Creek, Terrorism and Drug Trafficking, Economic and Commercial Cooperation, Peace and Security and Promotion of Friendly Exchanges in Various Fields) clearly demonstrate their commitment to the new reality and their determination to normalize the relationship with each other.
- As a part of their ongoing composite dialogue process, Indians and Pakistanis have met several times since 2004 to negotiate NRRMs with each other. This dialogue has, however, not made any significant headway. Given the present state of their relationship, incremental progress on this issue is more likely. If, however, Indo–Pakistan relations improve in future, progress can be expected along the lines identified by the Lahore MoU.
- To reduce nuclear dangers in the subcontinent, the people of both India and Pakistan must be made fully aware of the risks that go with possessing nuclear weapons. They should know that besides the risks of intentional, accidental, or unauthorized use of nuclear weapons, they are also dangerous even when 'at rest'.
- The US has established good relationships with both India

and Pakistan, and could play an important role. It could press Pakistan to dismantle the infrastructure of terrorism that it has used against India, encourage both New Delhi and Islamabad to accept a fair and reasonable solution to the Kashmir dispute, and, more importantly, assist both India and Pakistan in ensuring better security and control of their nuclear weapons and materials. Moreover, it could engage China in a discussion to seek its agreement to formalize the practice of storing warheads separately from ground-based missiles, and persuade Beijing to cease supplying advanced missile and nuclear technology to Pakistan. However, the US role will carry more weight if it pursues policies that contribute towards a more favourable global strategic environment.

Bibliography

PRIMARY SOURCES

'Additional Protocol to the Nuclear Non-Proliferation Treaty', at: http://www.spacewar.com/2003/031218114923.ghpco7d2.html

'Agreement between India and China on the Maintenance of Peace and Tranquillity Along the Line of Control (1993)', in *CBMs* in *South Asia: Potential and Possibilities*, ed. Dipankar Banerji, Colombo: RCSS, 2000, Appendix B, pp. 71–3.

'Agreement between the Government of the Republic of India and the Government of the People's Republic of China on Confidence Building Measures in the Military Field Along the Line of Actual Control in India–China Border Areas (1996)', in *CBMs in South Asia: Potential and Possibilities*, ed. Dipankar Banerji, Colombo: RCSS, 2000, Appendix C, pp. 74–80.

'Agreement between India and Pakistan on Prohibition of Attack Against Nuclear Installations and Facilities, 31 December 1988', at: http://www.indianembassy.org/South_Asia/pakistan/Prohibition_Attack_Nuclear_Dec_31

CCC Conference Report, 'Asymmetric Conflict in South Asia: The Causes and Consequences of the 1999 Limited War in Kargil', 29 May–1 June 2002, Monterey, California.

CIA, 'Global Trends 2015', 2001, at: http://www.odci.gov/cia/reports/globaltrends2015/index.html

'Comprehensive Nuclear Test Ban Treaty', at: http://www.armscontrol.org/DOCS/ctbttxt.htm

'Conventional Forces in Europe Treaty', at: http://www1.umn.edu/humanrts/peace/docs/conweaeurope.html

IAEA, 'Calculating the New Global Nuclear Terrorism Threat', *Strategic Digest*, vol. XXXI, no. 11, November 2001.

India, Government of, 'The Evolution of India's Nuclear Policy', reprinted in *India's Nuclear Deterrent: Pokhran II and Beyond*, ed. Amitabh Mattoo, New Delhi: Har-Anand Publishers, Government of India, 1998, Appendix II.

'India's Nuclear Forces, 2002', Bulletin of Atomic Scientists report at: http://www.thebulletin.org/issues/nukenotes/ma02nukenote.html

'India-Pakistan Agreement on Prevention of Air Space Violations and for Permitting Over-Flights and Landings by Military Aircraft, Apr 6, 1991', at: http://meadev.nic.in/Opn/kargil/air_agreement.htm

'India-Pakistan Agreement on Advance Notice on Military Exercises, Manoeuvres and Troop Movements, Apr 6, 1991', *Strategic Digest*, vol. 34, no. 6, June 2004.

'India–Pakistan Joint Statement on Nuclear Talks', *Indian Express*, 21 June 2004.

'Joint Statement, Second Round of India–Pakistan Expert Level Talks on Nuclear CBMs, 15 Dec, Islamabad', at: http://www.indianembassy.ru/docs-htm/en/in_05_04_t2412_2004.htm

'Joint Statement, India–Pakistan Expert Level Meeting on Conventional CBMs, Islamabad, 15 Dec 2004', at: http://www.indianembassy.ru/docs-htm/en/en_05_04_t2412_2004.htm

Kargil Commission Report at: http://alfa.nic.in.rs/general/25indi1.htm

Kargil Review Committee, *From Surprise to Reckoning. The Kargil Review Committee Report*, New Delhi: Sage, 2000.

Lok Sabha, 'Evolution of India's Policy', at: http://www.indianembassy.org/pic/nuclearpolicy.htm

National Security Advisory Board, 'India's Draft Nuclear Doctrine', 17 August 1999, at: http://www.indianembassy.org/policy/CTBT/nuclear_doctrine_aug_ 17_1999.html

Natural Resources Defence Council (NRDC), 'Consequences of Nuclear Conflict Between India and Pakistan', at: http://www.nrdc.org/nuclear/southasia.asp

'Pakistan's Nuclear Forces, 2001', NRDC Nuclear Notebook, *Bulletin of Atomic Scientists*, 7 June 2002, at: http://www.thebulletin.org/issues/nukenotes/jf02nukenote. html

Tenet, George, 'US Director of the CIA, Testimony to the US Congress', 2001, at: http://www.odci.gov/public_affairs/speeches/UNCLASSWWT_020/2001.html

'Text of the Lahore Declaration, Feb 21, 1999', at: http://www.indianembassy.org/South_Asia/Pakistan/lahoredeclaration.html

'Text of UN Resolution 1172 of 6 June 1998: After the Tests: US Policy Towards India and Pakistan', Report of the Independent Task Force, co-sponsored by the Brookings Institution, Washington, DC and The Council on Foreign Relations, New York, 1998, pp. 57–60.

'Nuclear Non-Proliferation Treaty', at: http://fas.org/nuke/control/npt/text/npt2.htm

SECONDARY SOURCES

Books

Arnett, Eric, ed., *Military Capacity and The Risk of War: China, India, Pakistan and Iran*, Oxford: Oxford University Press, 2000.

Bajpai, Kanti et al., eds., *Brasstacks and Beyond: Perception and Management of Crisis in South Asia*, New Delhi: Manohar, 1995.

Banerji, Dipankar, ed., *CBMs in South Asia, Potential and Possibilities*, Colombo: RCSS, 2000.

Bidwai, Praful and Achin Vanaik, *South Asia on a Short-Fuse: Nuclear Politics and the Future of Global Disarmament*, New Delhi: Oxford University Press, 1999.

Blair, Bruce G., *The Logic of Accidental Nuclear War*, Washington, DC: Brookings Institution, 1993.

Chari, P. R, Pervaiz Iqbal Cheema and Iftekharuzzaman, *Nuclear Non-Proliferation in India and Pakistan*, New Delhi: Manohar, 1996.

Chari, P. R., Sonika Gupta, Arpit Rajain, eds., *Nuclear Stability in South Asia*, New Delhi: Manohar, 2003.

Chellaney, Brahma, ed., *Securing India's Future in the New Millennium*, New Delhi: Orient Longman, 1999.

Chengappa, Raj, *Weapons of Peace: The Secret Story of India's Quest to Be a Nuclear Power*, New Delhi: HarperCollins, 2000.

Cohen, Stephen P., *The Indian Army: Its Contribution to the Development of a Nation*, Berkeley, CA: University of California Press, 1971.

——, *Nuclear Proliferation in South Asia*, Boulder, CO: Westview Press, 1991.

——, *The Pakistan Army*, Karachi: Oxford University Press, 1998.

Dossani, Rafiq and Henry Rown, eds., *Prospects for Peace in South Asia*, Stanford: Stanford University Press, 2005.

Dutt, Som, *India and the Bomb*, Adelphi Paper, Oxford: OUP, for IISS, 1966.

——, *The Defence of India's Northern Borders*, Adelphi Paper no. 25, London: IISS, 1996.

Feaver, Peter D., *Guarding the Guardians*, Ithaca: Cornell University Press, 1992.

Gagne, Chris and Michael Krepon, eds., *The Impact of Missile Defence on South Asia*, Washington, DC: Stimson Center, January 2004.

Ganguly, Sumit, *The Crisis in Kashmir: Portents of War, Hopes of Peace*, Cambridge, MA: Woodrow Wilson Center Press, 1999.

Hagerty, Devin T., *The Consequences of Nuclear Proliferation: Lessons from South Asia*, Cambridge, MA: MIT Press, 1998.

Hoffman, Stephen, *India and the China Crisis*, Berkeley: University of California Press, 1990.

Joeck, Neil, *Maintaining Nuclear Stability in South Asia*, Adelphi Paper, Oxford: OUP for IISS, 1997.

Jones, Rodney W. and Mark McDonough, with Toby F. Dalton and Gregory D. Koblentz, *Tracking Nuclear Proliferation: A Guide in Maps and Charts, 1998*, Washington, DC: Carnegie Endowment for International Peace/Brookings Institution Press, 1998.

Karnad, Bharat, ed., *Future Imperiled: India's Security in the 1990's and Beyond*, New Delhi: Viking Penguin, 1994.

Krepon, Michael and Mishi Faruqee, eds., *Conflict Prevention and Confidence Building Measures in South Asia: The 1990 Crisis*, Washington, DC: Stimson Center, 1994.

Krepon, Michael and Gagne, Chris, eds., *The Stability-Instability Paradox: Nuclear Weapons and Brinkmanship in South Asia*, Washington, DC: Stimson Center, June 2001.

Krepon, Michael and Haider, Zaid, eds., *Reducing Nuclear Danger in South Asia*, Washington, DC: Stimson Center, January 2004.

Malhotra, Vinay, *Nuclear and Missile Race in South Asia: Relevance of Military Restructuring*, New Delhi: Wisdom House, 2000.

McLean, Scila, ed., *China: How Nuclear Decisions are Made*, New York: St. Martin's Press, 1986.

Menon, Raja, *A Nuclear Strategy for India*, New Delhi: Sage, 2000.

Ramana, M.V. and C. Rammanohar Reddy, eds., *Prisons of the Nuclear Dream*, New Delhi: Orient Longman, 2003.

Mirchandani, G.G., *India's Nuclear Dilemma*, New Delhi: Popular Book Services, 1968.

Nair, Vijai K., *Nuclear India*, New Delhi: Lancer International, 1992.

Norris, Robert S., Andrew S. Burrows and Richard W. Fieldhouse, *Nuclear Weapons Databook*, vol. V: *British French, and Chinese Weapons*, Washington, DC: Natural Resources Defense Council, 1994.

Palit, D. K. and P.K.S. Namboodiri, *Pakistan's Islamic Bomb*, New Delhi: Vikas Publishing, 1979.

Paul, Jackson, ed., *Jane's All the World's Aircraft 2002–3*, Coulson, UK: Jane's Information Group, 2002.

Perkovich, George, *India's Nuclear Bomb: The Impact on Global Proliferation*, Berkeley: University of California Press, 1999.

Ramana, M.V., *Bombing Bombay: Effects of Nuclear Weapons and a Case Study of a Hypothetical Explosion*, Cambridge: International Physicians for the Prevention of Nuclear War, 1999.

Rehman, Shabidur, *Long Road to Chagai*, Islamabad: Print-Wise Publications, 1999.

Sagan, Scott D., *The Limits of Safely: Organisation, Accidents and Nuclear Weapons*, Princeton: Princeton University Press, 1993.

Sagan, Scott D. and Kenneth M. Waltz, *The Spread of Nuclear Weapons: A Debate*, New York: W.W. Norton, 1995.

Synnott, Hilary, *The Causes and Consequences of South Asia's Nuclear Tests*, Adelphi Paper, Oxford: OUP, for IISS, 1999.

Tellis, Ashley, *India's Emerging Nuclear Posture: Between Recessed Deterrent and Ready Arsenal*, Santa Monica: Rand, 2001.

——, *India's Emerging Nuclear Doctrine: Exemplifying the Lessons of the Nuclear Revolution*, Seattle: National Bureau of Asian Research, May 2001.

Tellis, Ashley, Christine C. Fair, and Jamison Jo Medby, *Limited Conflicts under the Nuclear Umbrella: Indian and Pakistani Lessons from the Kargil Crisis*, Santa Monica: Rand, 2001.

Thomas, Raju, and Amit Gupta, eds., *India's Nuclear Security*, New Delhi: Vistaar Publications, 2000.

Research Papers and Articles

Ahmad, Shamshad, 'The Nuclear Subcontinent: Bringing Stability to South Asia', *Foreign Affairs*, vol. 78, no. 4, July–August 1999.

Ahmed, Samina, 'Pakistan's Nuclear Weapons Programme', *International Security*, vol. 23, no. 4, Spring 1999.

——, 'The (Nuclear) Testing of Pakistan', *Current History*, vol. 97, no. 407, December 1998.

Albright, David, 'India and Pakistan's Fissilc Material and Nuclear Weapons Inventory, End of 1998', Washington, DC: ISIS, 27 October 1999, at: htpp://www.isisonline.org/publications/SouthAsia/stocks/000.html

Anand, Vinod, 'Contours of Pakistan's Nuclear Doctrine', *Strategic Analysis*, vol. XXIV, no. 3, June 2000.

Ansari, Massoud, 'Pakistan's Jihad Factories', *Frontline*, vol. 18, no. 16, 17 August 2001.

Arnett, Eric, 'Nuclear Stability and Arms Sales to India: Implications for U.S. Policy', *Arms Control Today*, vol. 27, no. 5, August 1997.

——, 'Conventional Arms Transfers and Nuclear Stability in South Asia', in *Nuclear Weapons and Arms Control in South Asia After the Test Ban*, ed. Arnett, Eric, Oxford: Oxford University Press, 1998.

Bailey, Kathleen and Satoshi Morimoto, 'A Proposal for a South Asian Intermediate Nuclear Forces Treaty', *Comparative Strategy*, no. 17, 1998.

Balchandran, G., 'How to Square the CTBT', *Strategic Analysis*, vol. XXV, no. 4, July 2000.

Bajpai, Kanti, 'The Fallacy of an Indian Deterrent', in India's Nuclear Deterrent: Pokhran II and Beyond, ed. Amitabh Mattoo, New Delhi: Har-Anand, 1999.

——, 'India's Nuclear Posture After Pokhran II', *International Studies*, vol. 37, no. 4, October–December 2000.

——, 'No First Use in the India-Pakistan Context', paper presented at the 279th Pugwash Meeting on South Asia, London, 15-17 November 2002.

Bajpai, K. Shankar, 'Untangling India and Pakistan', *Foreign Affairs*, vol. 82, no. 3, May–June 2003.

Basrur, Rajesh, 'Kargil, Terrorism and India's Strategic Shift', *India Review*, vol. 1, no. 4, October 2002.

——, 'Nuclear India at the Crossroads, *Arms Control Today*, vol. 33, no. 7, September 2003.

——, 'India's Escalation-Resistant Nuclear Posture' in *Escalation Control and the Nuclear Option in South Asia*, ed. Michael, Krepon, Rodney W. Jones and Ziad Haider, Washington, DC: Stimson Center, 2004, at: http://www.stimson.org/southasia/ pdf/ESCCONTROLCHAPTER3.pdf, pp. 1–19.

Basrur, Rajesh and Hasan Askari Rizvi, *Nuclear Terrorism and South Asia*, CMC Occasional Paper, February 2003, Albuquerque: Sandia National Laboratories.

Bedi, Rahul, 'A Credible Nuclear Deterrent?', *Frontline*, vol. 20, no. 7, 29 March–11 April 2003.

Behera, Ajay Darshan, 'The Supporting Structures for Pakistan's Proxy War in J&K', *Strategic Analysis*, vol. XXV, no. 3, June 2001.

Bhaskar, C. Uday, 'The May 1990 Nuclear "Crisis": An Indian Perspective', *Studies in Conflict and Terrorism*, vol. 20, no. 4, October–December 1997.

——, 'Nuclear Weapons and No-First Use; Need for Strategic Restraint', *Strategic Analysis*, vol. 24, no. 10, January 1998.

——, 'Bush Outlines New US Nuclear Policy', *Strategic Analysis*. vol. XXV, no. 3, June 2001.

Bidwai, Praful, 'Closing the Global Nuclear Bazaar, *Frontline*, vol. 21, no. 4, 27 February 2004.

Bowen, Clayton and Daniel Wolven, 'Command and Control Challenges in South Asia', *Non-Proliferation Review*, vol. 6, no. 3, Spring-Summer 1999.

Caldwell, Dan, 'Permissive Action Links: A Description and Proposal', *Survival*, May–June 1987.

Carranza, Mario E., 'An Impossible Game: Stable Nuclear Deterrence after the Indian and Pakistani Tests', *Non-Proliferation Review*, vol. 6, no. 3, Spring-Summer 1999.

Chari, P. R., 'India's Nuclear Doctrine: Confused Ambitions', *Non-Proliferation Review*, vol. 7, no. 3, Fall-Winter 2000.

Cheema, Zafar Iqbal, 'Pakistan's Nuclear Use Doctrine and Command and Control', in *Planning the Unthinkable: How New Powers Will Use Nuclear, Biological and Chemical Weapons*, ed. Peter R. Lavoy, Scott D. Sagan and James J. Witz, Ithaca, NY: Cornell University Press.

Chellaney, Brahma, 'South Asia's Passage to Nuclear Power', *International Security*, vol. 16, no. 1, Summer 1991.

——, 'After the Tests: India's Options', *Survival*, vol. 40, no. 4, 1998–9.

——, 'India's Nuclear Planning, Force Structure, Doctrine and Arms Control Posture', *Australian Journal of International Affairs*, vol. 53, no. 1, 1999.

Chengappa, Raj, 'Boosting the Arsenal', *India Today*, 29 February 1996.

——, 'Missiles: Boom for Boom', *India Today*, 26 April 1999.

——, 'If Pakistan Nukes India', *India Today*, 10 June 2002.

Cherian, John, 'Building Confidence', *Frontline*, vol. 21, no. 4, 16 July 2004.

Chitaranjan, Kalpana, 'State of the CTBT', *Strategic Analysis*, vol. 21, no. 4, June 2000.

Choudhury, Upendra, 'Security in a Period of Strategic Uncertainty: A Study of India's Ballistic Missile Programme', Ph.D. thesis, CPS/SSS, JNU, New Delhi, 1999.

——, 'Internal in Security Under Seize: Need for Constitutional Correctives', in *Reviewing the Constitution*, ed. B.L. Fadia, New Delhi: Himanshu Publishers, 2001.

——, 'Dealing With the Danger of Ballistic Missiles in South Asia', paper presented at the Graduate Conference on Amity and Enmity: Patterns of Peace, War and Insecurity in the 21st Century, Department of Politics and International Relations, Cartmel College, Lancaster University, Lancaster, England, 18 April 2002, at: http://www.ceip.org/files/projects/npp/pdf/SABM.pdf

——, 'Theatre Missile Defence: Implications for South Asian Security', *Journal of Peace Studies*, vol. 9, no. 5, July–August 2002.

——, 'Ballistic Missiles and India-Pakistan Strategic Balance', *Journal of Peace Studies*, vol. 9, no. 5, September–October 2002.

——, 'Too Close for Comfort', *Bulletin of Atomic Scientists*, vol. 59, no. 2, March–April 2003.

——, 'Nuclear Safety and Security Concerns in South Asia', paper presented at the 15th Summer Symposium on Science and World Affairs, 23–31 July 2003, Moscow.

Cirincione, Joseph, 'The Asian Nuclear Reaction Chain', *Foreign Policy*, Spring 2000.

Clary, Christopher, 'Dr Khan's Nuclear WalMart', *Disarmament Diplomacy*, no. 76, March—April 2004.

Cotta-Ramusino, Paolo and Maurizio Martellini, 'Nuclear Safety, Nuclear Stability and Nuclear Strategy in Pakistan', report of a visit by Landau Network-Centro-Volta, 21 January 2002, at: http://axmi.mi.infn.it/~landnet/Doc/pakistan.pdf

Dalton, Toby F., 'Toward Nuclear Rollback in South Asia', *Current History*, vol. 97, no. 412, December 1998.

Dubey, Muchkund, 'World Nuclear Order and India's Nuclear Deterrence', *Mainstream*, vol. XXXVI, no. 27, 27 June 1998.

Dunn, Lewis A., 'The Widening Nuclear Circle: South Asian Choices in Broader Perspective', in *Bridging the Non-Proliferation Divide*, ed. Francine Frankel, New Delhi: Konark Publishers, 1995.

——, 'Balancing Nuclear Security and Non-Proliferation in South Asia', in *A New Equation: US Policy Towards India and Pakistan After 11 September*, ed. Lee Feinstein, Carnegie Endowment for International Peace, May 2002.

Erickson, Andrew John, 'The Cuban Missile Crisis of 1962: Miscalculations, Escalation, and Near Nuclear Confrontation', Master's dissertation, Florida State University, 1994.

Feaver, Peter D., 'Command and Control in Emerging Nuclear Nations', *International Security*, Winter 1992–3.

Feaver, Peter D. and M.S. Niow Emerson, 'Managing Nuclear Proliferation: Condemn, Strike, or Assist', *International Studies Quarterly*, vol. 17, June 1996.

Feinstein, Lee, 'Avoiding Another Close Call in South Asia', *Disarmament Diplomacy*, no. 65, July–August 2002.

Fisher, Richard D., 'China Accelerates Navy Building', *China Brief*, vol. III, issue 15, 29 July 2003.

Ganguly, Sumit, 'Indo-Pakistani Nuclear Issues and the Stability-Instability Paradox', *Studies in Conflict and Terrorism*, vol. 18, 1995.

——, 'India's Pathway to Pokhran II: The Prospects and Sources of New Delhi's Nuclear Weapons Programme', *International Security*, vol. 23, no. 4, Spring 1999.

——, 'Behind India's Bomb: The Politics and Strategy of Nuclear Deterrence', *Foreign Affairs*, vol. 80, no. 5, September–October 2001.

Ganguly, Sumit and Kent Biringer, 'Nuclear Crisis Stability in South Asia', *Asian Survey*, vol. XLI, no. 6, November–December 2001.

Garver, John W., 'Asymmetrical Indian and Chinese Threat Perceptions', *Indian Review*, vol. 1, no. 4, October 2002.

Ghosh, P. K, 'Emerging Trends in the Nuclear Triad', *Strategic Analysis*, vol. XXV, no. 2, May 2001.

——, 'India-Pakistan Nuclear Parity: Is it Feasible or Necessary?', *Strategic Analysis*, vol. XXV, no. 4, July 2001.

Giles, Gregory F., 'Safeguarding the Undeclared Nuclear Arsenals', *Washington Quarterly*, Spring 1993.

Giles, Gregory F. and James Doyle, 'India and Pakistani Views on Nuclear Deterrence', *Comparative Strategy*, no. 15, 1996.

Goldstein, Avery, 'Great Expectations: Interpreting China's Arrival', *International Security*, vol. 22, no. 3, Winter 1997–8.

Gopalakrishnan, K.V., 'Are Nuclear Weapons that Bad?', *Indian Defence Review*, vol. 11, July September 1996.

Gregory, Jones, 'From Testing to Deploying Nuclear Forces: The Head Choices Facing India and Pakistan', Rand Paper 192, 2000, at: http://www.rand.org/publications/1p/1p192/

Gregory, Koblentz, 'Theatre Missile Defence and South Asia: A Volatile Mix', *Non-Proliferation Review*, vol. 4, no. 3, Spring-Summer 1997.

Gregory, Shaun, 'Nuclear Command and Control in South Asia', *Strategic Issues*, no. 3, Mar 2000, at: http://www.issi.org.pk/Nuclear%20Issues/N_NCA.htm

——, 'A Formidable Challenge: Nuclear Command and Control in South Asia', *Disarmament Diplomacy*, no. 54, February 2001.

Gronlund, Lisbeth, David Wright and Liu Yong, 'China and a Fissile Material Production Cut-Off', *Survival*, vol. 37, no. 4, Winter 1995–6.

Gupta, Amit, 'India's Draft Nuclear Doctrine', *Round Table*, vol. 355, July 2000.

——, 'South Asian Nuclear Choices: What Type of Force Structures May Emerge?', *Armed Forces Journal International*, September 1998.

Hagerty, Devin T., 'Nuclear Deterrence in South Asia: The 1990 Indo-Pakistani Crisis', *International Security*, vol. 20, no. 3, Winter 1995–6.

—— 'South Asia's Nuclear Balance', *Current History*, vol. 95, no. 165, April 1996.

Heisbourg, Francois, 'The Prospects of Nuclear Stability between India and Pakistan', Survival, vol. 40, no. 4, Winter 1998–9.

Hoodbhoy, Pervez, 'Pakistan's Nuclear Future', in *Pakistan and the Bomb: Public Opinion and Nuclear Choices*, ed. Samina Ahmed and David Cortright, Notre Dame: University of Notre Dame Press, 1998.

Hoyt, Timothy D., 'Pakistan's Nuclear Doctrine and Dangers of Strategic Myopia', *Asian Survey*, vol. XLI, no. 6, November–December 2001.

Hussain, Mushahid, 'Pakistan and the Nuclear Question', *National Development and Security*, August 1992.

Hussain, Zahid, 'Deliberate Nuclear Ambiguity', in *Pakistan and the Bomb: Public Opinion and Nuclear Choices*, ed. Samina Ahmed and David Cortright, Notre Dame: University of Notre Dame Press, 1998.

Ismat, Saeed, 'Strategy for Total Defence: A Conceptual Nuclear Doctrine', *Pakistan Defence Journal*, March 2000.

Jha, Prem Shankar, 'Why India Went Nuclear', *World Affairs*, vol. 2, no. 3, July–September 1998.

Jones, Rodney W., *Nuclear Proliferation: Islam, the Bomb, and South Asia*, CIS Washington Paper no. 82, Beverly Hills, CA: Sage, 1981.

——, 'Pakistan's Nuclear Posture: Arms Race Instabilities in South Asia', *Asian Affairs: An American Review*, vol. 25, no. 2, Summer 1998.

——, 'Pakistan's Nuclear Posture: Quest for Assured Nuclear Deterrence—A Conjecture', *Spotlight on Regional Affairs*, vol. XIX, no. 1, January 2000.

——,'Debating New Delhi's Nuclear Decision', *International Security*, vol. 24, no. 4, Spring 2000.

Joshi, Manoj, 'From Technology Demonstration to Assured Retaliation: The Making of an Indian Nuclear Doctrine', *Strategic Analysis*, vol. 22, no. 104, January 1998.

——, 'Safety Measures: Handle With Care', *India Today*, 2 November 1998.

——, 'The Indo-Pakistan Military Balance and Limited War', *Strategic Digest*, vol. 33, no. 1, January 2003.

Kalyanaraman, S., 'Operation Parakrama: An Indian Exercise in Coercive Diplomacy', *Strategic Analysis*, vol. 26, no. 4, December 2002.

Kamal, Nazir, 'Pakistani Perceptions and Prospects of Reducing the Nuclear Danger in South Asia', CMC paper at: http://www.cmc.sandia.gov/Links/about/papers/SAND98-0505/6/index.html

Kamath, P. K., 'Indian Nuclear Strategy: A Perspective for 2020', *Strategic Analysis*, vol. 22, no. 12, March 1999.

Kampani, Gaurav, 'From Existential to Minimum Deterrence: Explaining India's Decision to Test', *Non-Proliferation Review*, vol. 6, no. 1, Fall 1998.

——, 'Second Tier Proliferation: The Case of Pakistan and North Korea', *Non-Proliferation Review*, vol. 9, no. 3, Fall-Winter 2002.

Kanwal, Gurmeet, 'Does India Need Tactical Nuclear Weapons?', *Strategic Analysis*, vol. XXIV, no. 2, May 2000.

——, 'Nuclear Targeting Philosophy for India', *Strategic Analysis*, vol. 24, no. 3, June 2000.

——, 'India's Nuclear Force Structure', *Strategic Analysis*, vol. 24, no. 6, September 2000.

——, Nuclear Defence: Shaping the Indian Arsenal', *Indian Defence Review*, vol. 15, October–December 2000.

——, 'India's National Security in a Nuclear Environment', *Strategic Analysis*, vol. 24, no. 9, December 2000.

——, 'India's Nuclear Doctrine and Policy', Strategic Analysis, vol. XXIV, no. 11, February 2001.

Khakwani, Abdul Shakoor, 'Nuclear Proliferation in South Asia: A Case for the Regional Consensus', *Pakistan Horizon*, vol. 47, July 1994.

Khan, Feroz Hassan, 'Challenges to Nuclear Stability in South Asia', *Non-Proliferation Review*, vol. 10, no. 1, Spring 2003.

Khan, Munir Ahmed, 'Nuclearisation of South Asia and its Regional and Global Implications', *Focus on Regional Issues*, nos. 1–2, 1998.

Khan, Tanvir Ahmad, 'Command and Control: A Pakistani Perspective', *Strategic Issues*, no. 3, March 2000, at: http://www.issi.org.pk/Nuclear%20Issues/N_NCA. htm

Khurana, G. S, 'Proliferation Security Initiative: An Assessment', *Strategic Analysis*, vol. 28, no. 2, April–June 2004.

Koch, Andrew, 'Nuclear Power Submarine: India's Strategic Trump Card', *Jane's Intelligence Review*, June 1998.

Kraig, Michael Ryn, 'The Political and Strategic Imperatives of Nuclear Deterrence in South Asia', *India Review*, vol. 2, no. 1, January 2003.

Kumar, Anand, 'Role of CBMs in South Asia', *Journal of Peace Studies*, vol. 8, no. 2, March–April 2001.

Kumar, Satish, 'Militant Islam: The Nemesis of Pakistan, *Strategic Digest*, vol. XXX, no. 8, August 2000.

Kumar, Sumita, 'Pakistan's Jihadi Apparatus: Goals and Methods', *Strategic Analysis*, vol. XXIV, no. 2, March 2001.

Lahiri, Dilip, 'Formalising Restraint: The Case of South Asia', *Strategic Analysis*, vol. XXIII, no. 4, July 1999.

Lodhi, Maleeha, 'Security Challenges in South Asia', *Non-Proliferation Review*, vol. 8, no. 2, Summer 2001.

Mahmood, Tehmina, 'India and Pakistan's Nuclear Explosions: An Analysis', *Pakistan Horizon*, vol. 52, January 1999.

——, 'Kargil Crisis and Deteriorating Security Situation in South Asia', *Pakistan Horizon*, vol. 52, no. 4, October 1999.

Malik, Mohan, 'Nuclear Proliferation in Asia: The China Factor', *Australian Journal of International Affairs*, vol. 53, no. 1999.

Mansingh, Surjeet, 'India–China in the Post-Cold War Era', *Asian Survey*, vol. 34, no. 3, March 1994.

Mazari, Shirin M., 'Formulating a Regional Strategic Doctrine', Lahore: Pakistan Institute for Air Defence Studies, 1998.

McKinzi, Mathew, Zia Mian, M.V. Ramana and A.H. Nayyar, *Nuclear War in South Asia*, Foreign Policy in Focus Policy Report, New Mexico, June 2002.

Mehta, Pratap Bhanu, 'India: The Nuclear Politics of Self-Esteem', *Current History*, vol. 97, no. 623, December 1998.

Mian, Zia, 'Renouncing the Nuclear Option', in *Pakistan and the Bomb*, ed. Samina Ahmed and David Cortright, Notre Dame: University of Notre Dame Press, 1998.

Mian, Zia and M.V. Ramana, 'Beyond Lahore: From Transparency to Arms Control, *Economic and Political Weekly*, 17–24 April 1999.

Mian, Zia, M.V. Ramana and R. Rajaraman, 'Risks and Consequences of Nuclear Weapon Accidents in South Asia', *Current Science*, vol. 80, no. 10, 2001.

——, 'Yet Another Nuclear Danger', *Frontline*, vol. 18, no. 16, 17 August 2001.

Mian, Zia, A.H. Nayyar, and M.V. Ramana, 'Making Weapons Talking Peace: Resolving Dilemma of Nuclear Negotiations', *Economic and Political Weekly*, 17 July 2004.

Mishra, Ashutosh, 'India-Pakistan Talks 2004: Nuclear CBMs and Kashmir', *Strategic Analysis*, vol. 28, no. 2, April–June 2004.

Mohan, C. Raja, 'India's Nuclear Weapons and the Asian Balance', *Indian Defence Review*, vol. 13, July–September 1998.

——, 'The Nuclear Commandments', *World Focus*, vol. 19, nos. 10–12, October-December 1998.

——, 'No First Use and India's Nuclear Transition', paper presented at the 279th Pugwash Meeting on South Asia, London, 15–17 November 2002.

Naib, V.P., 'The Nuclear Threat', *Indian Defence Review*, vol. 8, no. 1, January 1993.

Naim, Rashid S., '*Aadhi Raat Ke Baad*' (After Midnight), in *Nuclear Proliferation in South Asia: The Prospects for Arms Control*, ed. Stephen Philip Cohen, Boulder, CO: Westview Press, 1999.

Norbu, Dawa, 'Tibet in Sino-Indian Relations: The Centrality of Marginality', *Asian Survey*, vol. 37, no. 11, November 1997.

Norris, Robert S. and Hans M. Kristensen, 'Chinese Nuclear Forces, 2003', *Bulletin of the Atomic Scientists*, vol. 59, no. 6, November–December 2003, at http://www.thebulletin. org/article_nn.php?art_ofn=nd03norris

Pattanaik, Smruti, 'Pakistan's Nuclear Strategy', *Strategic Analysis*, vol. 27, no. 1, January–March 2003.

Paul, T.V., 'The Systemic Bases of India's Challenges to the World Nuclear Order', *Non-Proliferation Review*, vol. 6, no. 1, Fall 1998.

——, 'Chinese-Pakistani Missile Ties and the Balance of Power', *Non-Proliferation Review*, vol. 10, no. 2, Summer 2003.

Perkovich, George, 'A Nuclear Third Way in South Asia', *Foreign Policy*, no. 91, Summer 1993.

Pregenzer, Arian L., 'Securing Nuclear Capabilities in India and Pakistan: Reducing the Terrorist and Proliferation Risks', *Non-Proliferation Review*, vol. 10, no. 1, Spring 2003.

Raghavan, R.K, 'Nuclear Terrorism', *Frontline*, vol. 20, no. 6, 15–28 March 2003.

Raghavan, V.R., 'Limited War and Nuclear Escalation in South Asia', *Non-Proliferation Review*, vol. 8, no. 3, Fall-Winter 2001.

Racine, Jean-Luc, 'Pakistan and the Indian Syndrome: Between Kashmir and the Nuclear Predicament', in *Pakistan: Nationalism Without a Nation?*, ed. Christophe Jaffrelot, New Delhi: Manohar, 2002.

Rajaraman, R., 'Nuclear Weapons in South Asia: Risks and Their Reduction', paper presented at the 277th Pugwash Workshop on South Asian Security, Geneva, 1–3 November 2002.

Rajaraman, R., M.V. Ramana and Zia Mian, 'Possession and Deployment of Nuclear Weapons in South Asia: An Assessment of Some Risks', *Economic and Political Weekly*, 22 June 2002, at: http://www.geocities.com/m_v_ramana/nucleararticles/epw_deploymentrisks.htm

Rajgopalan, Rajesh, 'Pakistan's Nuclear Export Initiative', *Strategic Analysis*, vol. 24, no. 6, September 2000.

Ramana, M.V. and A.H. Nayyar, 'India, Pakistan and the Bomb', *Scientific American*, December 2001.

Rappai, M.V., 'Nuclear Factor in India-China Relations', in *Asian Strategic Review*, ed. Jasjit Singh, New Delhi: IDSA, 1998–9.

——, 'China's Nuclear Arsenal and Missile Defence', *Strategic Analysis*, vol. 26, no. 1, January–March 2002.

Rauf, Tariq, 'Accommodation, Not Confrontation', *Bulletin of the Atomic Scientists*, vol. 55, no. 1, January–February 1999.

Raza, Maroof, 'Nuclear India's Doctrine of Deterrence', *Indian Defence Review*, vol. 14, July September 1999.

Reddy, B. Muralidhar, 'Hero Turned Victim', *Frontline*, vol. 21, no. 4, 27 February 2004.

——, 'Nuclear Home Truths', *Frontline*, vol. 21, no. 4, 27 February 2004.

Rehbein, Robert E., 'Managing Proliferation in South Asia: A Case for Assistance to Unsafe Nuclear Arsenals', *Non-Proliferation Review*, vol. 9, no. 1, Spring 2002.

Rehman, Shabidur, 'Nuclear Safety and Security in South Asia', in *Proliferation Challenges and Non-Proliferation Opportunity for New Administration*, ed. Michael Barletta, CNS Occasional Paper no. 4, MIIS, Monterey: Center for Non-Proliferation Studies, 2000.

——, 'Terrorism, Pakistan and Nuclear Weapons', in *After 9/11: Preventing Mass Destruction Terrorism and Weapons Proliferation*, ed. Michael Barletta, Monterey: Center for Non-Proliferation Studies, May 2002.

Rethinaraj, T.S. Gopi, 'Threats and Perceptions of Nuclear War in South Asia', *Swords and Ploughshares*, vol. XIV, no. 1, Summer 2002.

Rizvi, Hasan Askari, 'Pakistan's Nuclear Testing', *Asian Survey*, vol. XLI, no. 6, November–December 2001.

Roy, Arundhati, 'The End of Imagination', *Frontline*, vol. 15, no. 16, 1–14 August 1998.

Sachdev, A. K, 'Chinese Missiles: Winning the Limited War', *Strategic Analysis*, vol. XXIV, no. 3, June 2000.

——, 'India's Surface-to-Surface Missiles', *Strategic Analysis*, vol. XXIV, no. 2, May 2000.

Sagan, Scott D., 'The Perils of Proliferation in South Asia', *Asian Survey*, vol. XLI, no. 6, December 2001.

Sahgal, Arun and Singh, Tejinder, 'Nuclear Threat from China: An Appraisal', *Trishul*, vol. 6, no. 2, 1993.

Salik, Naeem Ahmad, 'Pakistan's Ballistic Missile Development Programme-Security Imperatives, Rationale and Objectives', *Strategic Studies*, vol. XXI, no. 1, Spring 2000.

Sattar, Abdul, 'Reducing Nuclear Dangers in South Asia: A Pakistani Perspective', *Non-Proliferation Review*, vol. 2, no. 2, Winter 1995.

Sawhney, Pravin, 'India, Pakistan and China: Need for a Missile Stabilisation Regime', paper presented at the annual Jane's Ballistic Missile Proliferation Conference, October 1999, London.

——, 'Pakistan Scores Over India in Ballistic Missile Race', *Jane's Intelligence Review*, November 2000.

Sen, Amartya, 'India and the Bomb', *Frontline*, vol. 17, no. 19, September 2000.

Seng, Jordan, 'Less is More: Command and Control Advantages of Minor Nuclear States', *Security Studies*, Summer 1997.

Shahi, Agha, 'Command and Control of Nuclear Weapons in South Asia', *Strategic Issues*, no. 3, March 2000, at: http://www.issi.org.pk/Nuclear%20Issues/N_NCA.htm

Shaikh, Farzana, 'Pakistan's Nuclear Bomb: Beyond the Non-Proliferation Regime', *International Affairs*, vol. 78, no. 1, 2000.

Shakoor, Farzana, 'Nuclearisation of South Asia and the Kashmir Dispute', *Pakistan Horizon*, vol. 51, no. 4, October 1998.

Shireen, Mazari, 'Comment: Nuclear Safety *vs.* Non-Proliferation', *Strategic Studies*, vol. XX, no. 20, Autumn 2000.

Sidhu, W.P.S., 'Pakistan Puts its Nuclear Cards on the Table', *Jane's Intelligence Review*, 10 July 1998.

——, 'India's Nuclear Use Doctrine', in *Planning the Unthinkable: How New Powers Will Use Nuclear Biological and Chemical Weapons*, ed. Peter R. Levoy, Scott D. Sagan and James J. Witz, Ithaca: Cornell University Press, 2000.

Singh, Jasjit, 'The Wars that Never Were', *India Today*, 28 February 1984.

——, 'A Nuclear Strategy for India', in *Nuclear India*, ed. Jasjit Singh, New Delhi: Knowledge World, 1998.

——, 'India's Nuclear Policy: The Year After', *Strategic Analysis*, vol. XXIII, no. 4, July 1999.

——, 'Dynamics of Limited War', *Strategic Analysis*, vol. XXIV, no. 7, October 2000.

——, 'Nuclear Command and Control', *Strategic Analysis*, vol. XXV, no. 2, May 2001.

Singh, Jaswant, 'Against Nuclear Apartheid', *Foreign Affairs*, vol. 77, no. 5, September–October 1998.

Singh, Swaran, 'China's Nuclear Weapons and Doctrine', in *Nuclear India*, ed. Jasjit Singh, New Delhi: Knowledge World, 1998.

Snyder, Glenn H., 'The Balance of Power and the Balance of Terror', in *The Balance of Power*, ed. Paul Seabury, San Francisco: Chandler, 1965.

Stern, Jessica, 'Pakistan's Jihad Culture', *Foreign Affairs*, vol. 79, no. 6, November–December 2000.

Subhas, Kapila, 'Pakistan Evades Core Issues in Nuclear CBMs Talks With India', South Asia Analysis Group at: http://www.saag.org/papers11/paper1041.html

Subrahmanyam, K., 'Nuclear Force Design and Minimum Deterrence Strategy for India', in *Future Imperilled*, ed. Bharat Karnad, New Delhi: Viking, 1994.

——, 'Nuclear India in Global Politics', *Strategic Digest*, vol. XXVIII, no. 2, December 1998.

——, 'India and the International Nuclear Order', in *Nuclear India in the Twenty-First Century*, ed. Sardesai, D.R. and Raju Thomas, New York: Palgrave, 2002.

Sakhuja, Vijay, 'Sea-Based Deterrence and Indian Security', *Strategic Analysis*, vol. XXV, no. 1, April 2001.

Sullivan, Michael J., 'Indian Attitudes on International Atomic Energy Controls', *Pacific Affairs*, Fall 1970.

Sundarji, K., *Effects of Nuclear Asymmetry on Conventional Deterrence*, Combat Paper no. 1, Mhow: College of Combat, 1981.

——, 'Nuclear Deterrence Doctrine for India', *Trishul*, vol. 5, no. 2, December 1992.

——, 'Imperatives of Indian Minimum Nuclear Deterrence', *Agni*, vol. 2, no. 1, May 1996.

Sundarji, K., 'Changing Military Equations in Asia: The Role of Nuclear Weapons', in *Bridging the Non-Proliferation Divide*, ed. Francine Frankel, New Delhi: Konark Publishers, 1995.

Talbott, Strobe, 'Dealing with the Bomb in South Asia, *Foreign Affairs*, vol. 78, no. 2, March–April 1999.

Tellis, Ashley J., 'Towards a Force-in-Being: The Logic, Structure and Utility of India's Emerging Nuclear Posture', *Strategic Studies* (special issue), India as an Emerging Power, vol. 25, no. 4, 2003.

Thomas, Raju, 'Whether Nuclear India?', in *Nuclear India in the Twenty-First Century*, ed. D. R. Sardesai, and Raju Thomas, New York: Palgrave, 2002.

Toor, Abdul Hameed, 'Technology and Operational Capabilities of Agosta 90B Submarine', paper presented at the 15th Summer Symposium on Science and World Affairs, 23–31 July 2003, Moscow.

Vanaik, Achin, 'Deterrence or a Deadly Game? Nuclear Propaganda and Reality in South Asia', *Disarmament Diplomacy*, no. 66, September 2002.

——, 'The Second Nuclear Age: Reducing Risk for the People of South Asia', *TNI Briefing Series*, no. 2004/2, Amsterdam.

Weiss, Leonard, 'Pakistan: It's Déjà Vu All Over Again', *Bulletin of Atomic Scientists*, vol. 60, no. 3, May–June 2004.

Winner, Andrew C. and Yoshihara Toshi, *Nuclear Stability in South Asia*, IFPA, Spring 2002, at: http://www.ifpa.org/pdf/nssa.pdf

Yasmeen, Samina, 'Pakistan's Nuclear Tests: Domestic Debate and International Determinants', *Australian Journal of International Affairs*, vol. 53, no. 1, 1999.

Yuan, Jing-dong, 'India's Rise After Pokhran II', *Asian Survey*, vol. XLI, no. 6, November–December 2001.

Zahra, Farah, 'Pakistan's Road to a Minimum Nuclear Deterrent', *Arms Control Today*, vol. 29, no. 5, July–August 1999.

Zhang, Ming, 'China's Changing Nuclear Posture: Reactions to the South Asian Nuclear Tests', Carnegie Endowment for International Peace Paper, Washington, DC, 1999, at: http://www.ceip.org/pubs/china-zhang/CH2.PDF

——, 'What Threat?', *Bulletin of Atomic Scientists*, vol. 55, no. 5, September–October 1999.

Zhengiang, Pan, 'On Chinese NFU of Nuclear Weapons', paper presented at the 279th Pugwash Meeting on South Asia, London, 15–17 November 2002.

Zuberi, Martin, 'Safety of Pak Nukes', *World Focus*, vol. 22, nos. 10–12, October–December 2001.

RCSS PUBLICATIONS

- *Defence, Technology and Cooperative Security in South Asia: Report on the Proceedings of the Tenth Summer Workshop* (RCSS, 2004)
- *Environment Development and Human Security: Perspectives from South Asia* (2003)
- *Terrorism in South Asia: Impact on Development and Democratic Process* (SIPRA, 2003)
- *South Asia and the War on Terrorism* (India Research Press, 2003)
- *Shaping the Future—A South Asian Civil Society Dialogue* (RCSS, July 2002)
- *Small Arms and Human Insecurity* (RCSS, July 2002)
- *SAARC in the Twenty-First Century: Towards a Cooperative Future* (July 2002)
- *Memories of a Genocidal Partition: The Haunting Tale of Victims, Witnesses and Perpetrators* (RCSS, July 2002)
- *South Asian Security Futures: A Dialogue of Director's Regional Strategic Studies Institutes* (March 2002)
- *Security and Governance in South Asia* (September 2001)
- *Globalization and Non-Traditional Security in South Asia* (September 2001)
- *Security in the New Millennium* (India Research Press, 2001)
- *The Simla Agreement 1972—Its Wasted Promise* (Manohar, 2001)

RCSS Newsletter

A quarterly bulletin, it publishes a brief report of RCSS activities, presentations at its workshops on topics of contemporary interest and news and programmes of the RCSS and its alumnae.

RCSS Policy Studies

35 Nuclear Risk Reduction Measures in South Asia: Problems and Prospects (Manohar, 2005)
34 Indo-Pak Conflicts: Ripe to Resolve? (Manohar, 2005)
33 Small Arms and the Security Debate in South Asia (Manohar, 2005)
32 New Nuclear Triangle and China's Role in South Asia (RCSS, 2005)
31 Stability through Economic Cooperation in a Nuclear Environment (Manohar, 2005)
30 Multi-Track Diplomacy between India and Pakistan: A Conceptual Framework for Sustainable Security (Manohar, 2005)
29 The Role of Mediation in Resolving India-Pakistan Conflict: Parameters and Possibilities (Manohar, 2005)
28 HIV/AIDS as a Security Threat to India (Manohar, 2005)
27 Nepal's Maoist Movement and Implications for India and China (Manohar, 2005)
26 Elite Perceptions in Foreign Policy: Role of Print Media in Influencing India-Pakistan Relations, 1989–1999 (Manohar, 2004)
25 Nuclar Risk Reduction Measures and Restraint Regime in South Asia (Manohar, 2004)
24 River Water Sharing Problem Between India and Pakistan: Case Study of the Indus Basin Water Treaty (June 2004)
23 Christianity and Political Conflict in India: The Case of Gujarat (June 2002)

Fellowship in South Asian Alternatives (FISAA) Monograph

- Water, Power And People: A South Asian Manifesto on the Politics and Knowledge of Water (1997)
- The Nuclear Debate: Ironies and Immoralities (1998)

Others

- *Directory of Individuals and Institutions Engaged in South Asian Strategic Studies* (1998).